Men on
MIDLIFE

Eighteen Men Talk About Making New Choices in Careers, Relationships, and What Really Matters in the Second Half of Life

Barbara Thomas

Joanne Vickers, Ph.D.
Barbara L. Thomas, M.S.Ed.

THE CROSSING PRESS
FREEDOM, CALIFORNIA

Copyright ©
Cover design I
Printed in the

For information on bulk purchases or group discounts for this and other Crossing Press titles, please contact our Special Sales Manager at 800-777-1048.

Library of Congress Cataloging-in-Publication Data

Men on Midlife: eighteen men talk bout making new choices in careers, relationships, and what really matters in the second half of life/ [interviews by] Joanne Vickers, Barbara L. Thomas.
    p. cm.
    Includes bibliographical references.
    ISBN 0-89594-812-5 (pbk.)
    1. Middle aged men--United States. 2. Middle aged men--United States--case studies. 3. Middle age--United States. 4. Life cycle, Human. I. Vickers, Joanne F. II.Thomas, Barbara L. (Barbara Lee), 1939-
HQ1059.5.U5M449 1996
305.24'4--dc20   96-22339
                                                              CIP

Contents

Acknowledgments

We would like to thank the many men who have generously shared their stories and their lives with us. They have made us appreciate how difficult it is to be a man in today's world. Their willingness to talk and to trust has affected us deeply.

We want to thank Chris Bates, Kay Bonham, Marti and Ron Bruder, Bill Carroll, Pat Clarke, Lou DeWein, Pat Doust, Jennifer Diederich, David Lenfest, Richard North, Liz Noe, Rita Planitzer, Mick Ratliff, Bill Vensel, Robert Westerfelhaus, and Jan Williamson for reading various drafts of the manuscript.

We are grateful to Joe Amato, Anne Crimmings, Crazy Ladies Book Store, Michael Daniels, John Diederich, Jr., Nancy and Hugh Edgar, Andy Grace, Carol Haueter, Sandra Joblonicky, Arthur Middleton, Jim and Sandy Polen, and Gus Thomas for their hospitality, support, and suggestions.

Cecil Benoit, Marti Bruder, Jackie Chichester, Lou DeWein, Steve Einstein, Alan Gilberg, Jackie Gilchrist, Mary Goff, David Lenfest, Susan Linden, Jim Polen, Rita Park, Bobbie Stynes, and Gaylon Vickers graciously provided us with names of men they thought we should interview.

We would like to thank the various men's groups in Columbus, Ohio; Santa Fe, New Mexico; and Washington, D.C. for their support and encouragement.

We are grateful to our families for their patience and understanding as we developed this manuscript over the last three years.

Finally, we would like to thank Elaine Goldman Gill and the staff of The Crossing Press, especially Ron Stringer, our copy editor, for their faith in this project.

Preface

The history of a civilization is written in the stories of its real and mythic heroes. These stories recount the lives of men of strength, courage, skill, and intelligence who have accomplished admirable, even incredible deeds. Depending on the time and the cultural context, such heroes have slain dragons and saved princesses, conquered the elements and discovered the North Pole, or spent years starving in a garret to produce a masterpiece.

By virtue of their gender, girls have traditionally been socialized onto the sidelines of these stories, in which women appear mostly as supporters and observers. But tales about heroes have been handed to boys as both a challenge and an expectation: If he can kill the enemy, discover a continent, build an empire, bat .400, so can you. You can control, compete, win. Such is the power of heroic myth.

A closer look at these stories, however, reveals certain flaws of omission or minimalization that have important consequences. These stories don't, for the most part, develop the emotional or introspective dimensions of the characters. Neither do they elaborate on their characters' anxieties; if these are dealt with at all, it is as hurdles over which the heroes must jump on their various paths to glory.

It's no surprise, then, that by the time they have become adults, many men have no cultural text to validate either their feelings or their doubts about their psychological and physical abilities. Such is the power of heroic myth that it challenges men to become gods.

Perhaps an even more fundamental problem with stories of popular heroes is that they have overwhelmed the stories of ordinary people, the "casts of thousands" who have fallen under their shadows for centuries. Only within recent history has this tradition begun to change. Contemporary arts and media have highlighted stories of ordinary people, lending them both validity and public value. An American example is Willy Loman, the "hero" of Arthur Miller's 1949 play *Death of a Salesman*. More recently, Ken Burns' documentary on the Civil War incorporated the diaries and journals of private citizens and common soldiers, providing a picture of how that war affected the ordinary people of both the North and the South.

Whether or not we're famous, all of us have a story, and that story is important. It is the architecture of our experience; it gives shape to our lives and to the memories of our lives. Telling our stories helps us to define ourselves, and knowing who we are allows us to recognize ourselves as worthy of respect. In his book *Care of the Soul* (Harper Collins, 1992), Thomas Moore claims a spiritual value for personal stories when he says that storytelling helps us see the themes that circle in our lives and is therefore an excellent way of caring for our souls.

In the process of writing this book, we interviewed one hundred men roughly between the ages of forty and sixty who come from different ethnic, educational, social, economic, and geographic backgrounds. We found these men through a process of "convenient selection." Friends and coworkers would say, "If you get to San Antonio, you should call my brother," or "If you're going to Portland, I know a guy there who is pretty interesting."

We also used media personnel and local chambers of commerce as resources. We looked up a couple of men we had gone to high school with because we wondered what had become of them. We even accosted men we met (it *felt* like accosting sometimes) when they repaired our cars or our air conditioners, or sold us gifts at a tourist site.

The idea for writing *Men on Midlife: Eighteen* Men *Talk About Making New Choices in Careers, Relationships, and What Really Matters in the Second Half of Life* came, naturally enough, while we were writing *No More Frogs, No More Princes: Women Making Creative Choices at Midlife* (The Crossing Press, 1993). As we listened to women between forty and sixty talk about their life experiences, about how they had changed from the time they were children to their middle years, we wondered about some important people in our lives—the boys we had played with, then dated; the men we had married, and the men we counted as good friends; the sons we had raised.

As we remembered them, the boys we knew when we were growing up seemed to us to have "had it together." They had almost always looked self-contained and confident, as though they knew what they were doing. We discussed how difficult marriage often is because of the discrepant ways men and women deal with their feelings. And we shared concerns about our grown sons, who often appear to limit their expression of emotions.

When we talked with several friends of both sexes about our intention of interviewing midlife men for a book, they warned us that men probably wouldn't talk with us or that they wouldn't open up and be honest with us. With a few exceptions, we have not found this to be true. Once the men understood that we were not writing a male-bashing book and that we were sincere in wanting to provide a forum for their personal stories, they were, by and large, able to speak from the heart about their lives.

The structure of our interviews was open-ended. We asked men to tell us their life stories, starting with what their childhoods and growing up years had been like. We asked them to tell us what had happened to them as young men and how they had come to view themselves as midlife men. We encouraged them to talk about the important events and significant people in their lives. We were also interested in who their role models had been and in what messages about being a man they had received while they were growing up.

Often, the process of the interviews was much like peeling an onion. At first, the men tended to summarize the factual milestones of their lives, excluding the details of what they had done or how they had felt about what was happening to them. The stories would go something like this: "I was born…I graduated from school…then got married and had kids…changed jobs once or twice…and here I am."

The longer the men talked, however, the more comfortable they became, and the more they remembered about their experiences. Men who started out the interview holding their bodies tensely and looking away from us ended up by relaxing and maintaining eye contact. Many interviews lasted as long as two-and-a-half hours. Often enough, we reinterviewed subjects.

At the end of the interviews, men frequently admitted that they had not anticipated revealing so much of themselves. A few told us bluntly that they had decided in advance not to say much at all. For example, one man admitted ruefully, "I only planned to talk with you for an hour. I don't like talking about myself at all—that's psychology stuff! Now it's so late I don't know if I'll be able to get up tomorrow in time for my golf game."

The Introduction will elaborate on the themes we discovered from our interviews in the context of men's socialization process and their midlife experiences. It is followed by eighteen representative autobiographical accounts from this group.

Although our subjects were generous in telling us their personal stories, they did so with the understanding that their identities would be protected.

We have used pseudonyms—and changed locations in a few instances—to protect their confidentiality. When we have used their real names, we have said so in the introductions to the interviews.

We feel privileged to have listened to these men as they reflected on their lives. We want *Men on Midlife: Eighteen Men Talk About Making New Choices in Careers, Relationships, and What Really Matters in the Second Half of Life* to honor men's lives, and to serve as a voice for the men who read these stories as well as for those who actually spoke with us. We also hope that this book will help to build a bridge between men and women, so that all of us can listen to one another from the heart.

Introduction

Mention the term "male midlife crisis" in a conversation, and you're likely to get an arch look accompanied by remarks about gold chains, fast sports cars, and nubile blondes. It's a term that suggests irresponsibility and desperation, implying that a man who has not achieved his goal in life is so afraid of failure that he wants to forget everything that might remind him of it—especially the fact that he is getting older.

This stereotype of male midlife crisis lurks around the edges of men's consciousness as they approach middle age. It can produce real anxiety as they consider changes in their careers, relationships, and lifestyles. Still, as they approach their forties, most men do feel a real and legitimate need to make changes in their lives, although for the great majority, these changes are not the melodramatic stuff of the midlife-crisis stereotype.

What are these changes, how and why do they occur, and what are the consequences for midlife men and the people with whom they have relationships? That's what we set out to discover three years ago when we started interviewing men. Listening to more than one hundred stories gave us answers that made us see our male contemporaries with new eyes.

The answers begin in the American cultural environment of the 1940s and '50s. For men who grew up in this era, life seemed simpler than it does today. Issues could be more easily weighed in terms of black and white. Families were idealized along the lines of the TV show *Father Knows Best*. Messages about masculinity emphasized power and achievement, personal sacrifice, and self-control. Good-guy heroes like John Wayne and Superman dominated movie screens, and comic books, and the hearts of young boys. Almost everyone believed that if a man worked hard, his reward was certain. These men have experienced what has been called the "masculine mystique."

The relative simplicity and certainty of this era is reflected in the childhood memories of midlife men. In our interviews, we were struck by the detailed reminiscences so many men had of their childhoods. They often spoke with great enthusiasm about what they had done, where they had gone, the games they had played, and who their friends had been. They talked about being spontaneous, adventurous, and creative. They had been free to dream, to explore their environments, and to express their emotions. ("[I remember] days in the summertime that just went on forever"; "[I] grew up enjoying walking through the woods and...getting lost in cornfields and building forts in the barn.")

By the time they reached adolescence, however, the problematic reality of becoming male had begun to replace the romance of childhood. Some of our subjects spoke about their confusion as adolescents. They felt that they had never received clear messages about becoming men from appropriate adult figures. They spoke with regret about not having a supportive initiation into manhood.

John A. Sanford and George Lough confirm such difficulties of male adolescence in their book, *What Men Are Like* (Paulist Press, 1988): "[Adolescence] is a period of trial...Many men do not feel adequately initiated into manhood and never do feel in possession of their masculinity...[Consequently,] they feel they must repeatedly prove themselves as men."

The socialization process undergone by most men gradually molded them into acceptable "types" of manhood that left little room for their spontaneity and channeled their abilities into narrow production-achievement outlets. They heard the same messages from parents, teachers, and coaches: "Big boys don't cry," "Don't be a sissy," "Work hard if you want to amount to something," "Don't let anybody get the best of you." They learned to compete, achieve, and win. They learned to stop crying, to stuff their emotions. Their access to a full range of feelings was gradually, but systematically, shut off.

In effect, the messages had taught them that becoming a man was a precarious task. You didn't just grow into manhood; you had to prove yourself worthy of it. You dare not fail the test, on the sandlot or in the science lab. And if, for some unmentionable reason, you did fail, you couldn't let yourself feel bad about it, or tell anyone about it. You had to stiffen your resolve, keep control of yourself, try harder. Heroes in the making.

The socialization process for males almost always involves separation from mothers and identification with fathers. Nevertheless, it surprised us how few of our subjects spoke about their mothers; fewer yet described having a close relationship with their mothers. On the other hand, most of these men spoke at great length about the development of their relationships—positive and negative—with their fathers.

Our subjects' descriptions of their fathers were fairly uniform. Their fathers were men who had survived the economic and psychological hardships of the Great Depression, men who had clear ideas about their roles. It was their responsibility to bring home enough money to support their families; the rest was up to their wives. For the children, Father's word was law. He wasn't much interested in the niceties of communication or the subtleties of emotion. Accordingly, these fathers passed their work ethic, their attitudes about family responsibility, and their communicative and emotive styles on to their sons.

Some of our subjects credited their fathers with teaching them various skills, such as how to drive and fix a car, hunt for rabbits, or develop a successful business. Some acknowledged the values their fathers had taught them: responsibility, determination, providing for a family.

In contrast, other subjects spoke at length about the physical and psychological abuse they had received from their fathers. A forty-year-old opera singer recalled: "My father couldn't deal with my overzealous personality. He would try to get me under control and keep me from embarrassing him. If I was a little too loud or rambunctious, he'd say, 'Cool it. Keep your voice down'." Another man described the "board of education" with which his father beat him so badly he couldn't sit down afterwards.

Indeed, fathers loom so large in their sons' stories that it wasn't unusual for the men we interviewed to begin by telling us their fathers' stories. Quite often, men described some facet of their own lives by drawing upon a similar facet of their fathers' lives.

By the time our subjects reached adulthood, most of them had completed a gender training that had shaped them into corporate hunters and warriors. Denied the opportunity to develop tempering qualities of compassion, trust, and vulnerability, men can become isolated from others and from their own full range of feelings. They knew how to be active, aggressive, independent, competitive problem-solvers. For many men, the only acceptable emotion was anger, which often exploded inappropriately. They understood the value of power and money. They knew their duty—to support and protect the women and children.

They were expert at suppressing any fears or doubts about their manliness; consequently, these insecurities had never been resolved. As one physician explained: "I put [my emotions] in boxes, and I put the boxes up on shelves. If something's really tough to deal with—like a death in the family—then the lid of that box is really tight, and it goes way up there on some shelf." Such attitudes had been encouraged, tacitly perhaps, by other men and by women whose socialization had emphasized both supporting their mates' endeavors and assuming responsibility for the emotional content of their relationships.

It seems clear, too, that the men we interviewed were shaped by a complex modern society that does not promote introspection or self-reflection, that provides few mentors and models for change as they grow older. Men are encouraged to climb the corporate ladder rather than to sit quietly for a while on one of the ladder's rungs. They are encouraged to support their families financially rather than to spend time at home.

When men approach their middle years, however, most have begun to question their roles as producers, problem-solvers, and protectors. For some, this evaluation follows a dramatic change in the circumstances of their lives, such as divorce, illness, job loss, or the birth of a child. Occasionally, a wife's determination to change her own life will cause a husband to take a personal inventory. Still other men become aware of a confusing but persistent discomfort about "doing more and enjoying it less." They may find themselves drinking more than usual, becoming increasingly irritable, or experiencing chronic fatigue and vague symptoms of illness or depression. Being a hero all the time is hard work.

If a realized human being may be described as one who fully develops his or her intellectual, physical, emotional, spiritual, and social abilities, then these men have been denied the opportunity to develop their human potential. Midlife seems to be the time in which many men awaken to this potential.

The process of midlife awakening varies. Some men spend serious time analyzing their lifestyle, how it has developed and how they want to change it. They may enter therapy for a time. They may seek the company of others in a men's group or in a twelve-step fellowship. They may search out times and settings where they can enjoy solitude and the simple pleasures of nature. Some will act out their feelings of frustration and failure through various inappropriate behaviors. Other men, resistant or unused to self-reflection, may act more intuitively to make changes in their lives, sensing their way to new, more satisfying ways of being.

Although every individual deals with this process of questioning and awakening differently, our interviews did reveal a few persistent patterns. When men embark on a new journey during midlife, it's almost always a journey inward to rediscover parts of themselves that have been lost. They follow a trail that puts them in touch with the boy within, integrating this boy into their lives in a way that helps them achieve an authentic manhood or, as one contributor to David Lenfest's book, *Men Speak Out* (Health Communications, 1991), states it, a "creative masculinity." Some men, however, perhaps fearful of losing the identity they have maintained for so long, refuse to look long and hard at their lives; they retrench and try to continue on as they have done.

Because men's socialization has discouraged them from developing either the habit of feelings or a language with which to express their feelings, a significant part of their midlife journey focuses on emotional development. They strive to recapture the emotional freedom of the boy within—the boy who cried when he got hurt, who yelled his joy when he won a game, or freely hugged his friends and siblings in affection. This does not mean that they become childish or act childishly; it involves peeling off the various socialized layers of working, achieving, and providing to get down to a feeling core, which they reintegrate into their identity.

In this context, many men talked about their need for "permission" to express their feelings. When we asked who they needed permission from, they answered "society," meaning their male and female peers. (It wasn't enough to get permission from the woman with whom they had a relationship, because they feared that this permission might carry with it a hidden agenda or might be withdrawn capriciously.)

Another important part of the inner child that midlife men reclaim is a capacity for enjoyment, spontaneity, and creativity. In other words, many men get back in touch with their need to do things because they want to do them, because an activity is personally satisfying—not because society says they ought to.

Midlife men's reintegration of the inner child's capacity to feel and to be emotionally self-fulfilled occurs in a variety of contexts. For example, several of the men we interviewed described how they had learned to love deeply and to enjoy demonstrating their love with children they had during midlife. Some men talked about the deepened capacity for love and communication they developed in a second marriage after recovering from the devastation of a divorce. Similarly, some men revitalized their commitment to a first marriage.

A few talked about learning to love themselves, to realize that they were valuable as individuals, not only as part of a relationship or because of what they had achieved. Many of these men had learned to enjoy the solitude of living alone and doing what they wanted for the first time in their lives. Other men talked about the brotherly affection they began to develop and value as they participated in a men's group. Men's groups build on mutual trust among members who validate the caring part of themselves. As one man explained, "We don't come together to exclude women. We come together to heal ourselves."

For men in their fifties who are part of a men's group, mentoring younger men and boys can be an important outgrowth of their own healing. Some groups design ceremonies that honor older men as elders as well as male initiation rituals for adolescents. Some become involved in community outreach programs with younger males.

A Santa Fe jeweler described his group's involvement with high school boys: "One guy was into drugs and alcohol. Where is he now? A full-paid scholarship at a top-notch university. And he's wrestling—he figured out that he was a good wrestler. We got him off drugs. We became his mentors. This is part of the energy that is being developed by a superb group of older men."

Some men told us stories about how they had awakened at midlife to realize how stifling their jobs or environments had become. They had decided to embark on new careers or move to more congenial locations. If, for some reason, they could not make significant changes in their jobs or environments, they became involved in satisfying hobbies and other recreational interests, such as fishing, photography, and pottery making.

Again, the motivation for such changes seemed to stem from a need to recover and develop a part of themselves to which they had not given expression since boyhood. Such changes contribute to their development as authentic men who allow themselves a fuller range of expression.

Some men, as part of the traditional socialization process, develop critical skills that they are able to put to use in their middle years. Since boyhood, they have been taught to take risks and to survive the consequences of taking risks. They have also learned to be action-oriented. At midlife, they apply these skills to reintegrating the capacity for feeling and self-fulfillment possessed by the boy within.

We talked with many men who have taken risks to achieve personal growth. They seem easier with themselves, with the people they are connected to, and with the world in general. As one man explained, "If you've lived fifty years, you've done a lot of monumental living. If something sad is happening, it's still sad, but it's buffered by other events in life that say, 'Things go on.' There's enough to draw upon by now in my life to allow me to put things in perspective. I'm comfortable with this."

Such men are more comfortable not only with their feelings, but with talking about their feelings. This, in turn, helps them develop relationships with others that are more open and that acknowledge both parties' needs and interests.

Similarly, some men spoke of a knowledge or wisdom they had acquired through being at peace with themselves. They have come to a settled acceptance of life in general and their own lives in particular. They have achieved a sharper sense of connectedness with the environment and with others.

For example, a store manager explained how he had learned to experience life instead of forcing it. A photographer claimed, "I love getting older. I think it's because of the knowledge. I like to think I make better decisions." The abbot of a Catholic monastery told us, "If I find myself getting uptight, part of the wisdom I've learned is [that] my reactions are mine and I'm responsible for them...If I get angry with a brother, even if he's doing something objectively wrong, my anger is my problem. My impatience is my problem." An entrepreneur spoke of committing his time and financial resources to saving the rainforests of the world.

In *Hero With a Thousand Faces* (Princeton University Press, rev. ed., 1990), Joseph Campbell summarizes the character and quest of the hero as mythologized in cultures all over the world for thousands of years. Two common points in these tales are the hero's initial restlessness due to his sense that something is missing in his life and the hero's response to the call to adventure.

Modern midlife men are offering new interpretations to traditional heroic myths. Their quest begins with the often painful recognition that something essential is missing in their definitions of themselves. Their journey requires of them the courage to break from the past and persist through a dark country of many uncertainties and fears, often with few external guideposts. Like Luke Skywalker, they must learn to reach out with their feelings.

At journey's end, what these men discover is an expanded ability to nourish and honor all parts of themselves. With this awakened sense of who they are, they begin to develop honest and intimate relationships with others and with their environment. The stories that follow illustrate the journeys and accomplishments of these new heroes.

A Kid from Brooklyn

Jake Behar

I think something happens, at least for someone like
myself, as you get older. I was much more driven when
I was younger. I would do anything for a story. Anything.
I'd go anyplace, stay up for two days and go into an area
where there were violent riots. I was driven. I wanted that
kind of success. Now I feel much more at ease.

If someone were to say to me, "Wouldn't you like to go to
Bosnia and cover that civil way," I'd say, "Go fly a kite."
Give me a quiet mountaintop and an open can of beer. I'll
be happy as anything.

*It is a summer morning in the late 1940s. A poor Jewish boy, wide-eyed and
street-smart, steps out onto the street from the three-story apartment building where he lives with his family. He looks up and down the street for his
friends as he climbs onto his bike. The fragrances of baking bread and
kosher pickles mix with the dusty smell of Brooklyn, forming an enduring
imprint on the boy's memory.*

*Jake Behar, a fifty-two-year-old freelance writer now living in Colorado,
describes his childhood with colorful imagery. He grew up in an ethnic
neighborhood of Jewish immigrants. Although his father was never able to
provide very well for the family, Jake describes a childhood rich in ethnic
traditions and cultural experiences. These early exposures helped form the
basis for his eclectic interests and zest for living.*

*Several relationships along the way were also key: an older brother who
introduced him to music and backpacking, a high school teacher who
guided his reading, and a high school sweetheart who loved his different-
ness, and became his wife and lifelong friend.*

*Even an interesting and successful career and family life, however, did
not forestall a midlife crisis. Jake fell prey to the stagnation and deadened
emotions that many people experience in their long-term relationships.
Looking for an answer outside himself led to a serious affair. Two years
later, he experienced a moment of clarity about his personal values while
he was attending a funeral; this eventually resulted in a new commitment*

to his marriage. Working through this confusing period also involved a redefinition of the marriage.

Several years later, at age fifty, Jake realized that he felt like a "crazy man" under the unrelenting pressure of a job that he knew he was being forced out of. But this period also provided an opportunity to consider what he valued most in his life and led him to create more satisfying work.

In the process of examining his life, Jake was able to reintegrate some of the rich experience of his boyhood. He enjoys the "boy within" in fresh contexts, through such ordinary activities as riding his bike, being with his wife, pursuing his interest in music, and celebrating his Jewish heritage. Jake's new career as a freelance writer has afforded him the freedom to pursue meaningful relationships and activities.

I was born in Coney Island in 1941. My father was a Spanish Jew from Turkey who came over to the United States illegally, by way of Cuba, when he was eighteen. Many Sephardic Jews, especially of that generation, spoke Ladino, a dialect of fifteenth-century Spanish. So he was able to communicate in Cuba, even though his Spanish probably sounded strange.

When he came here, he basically made a living for himself doing odds and ends—and evidently was fairly successful, my brother says, until he had this accident when he was working on a garbage truck. He slipped and hit his head.

My mother wouldn't let them do surgery, but they told her that whatever this damage was might result in his being belligerent or unstable at times. That's my brother's explanation for why my father was the way he was. I have no idea if any of that's accurate. But I know that I didn't have much of a relationship with him.

I can remember occasionally playing catch with him down the middle of the street. And I remember sometimes, if he had some money, he'd slip a quarter or half-buck into my hand, but he'd always do it very secretively, like this was a big deal. Other than that, I don't have positive pictures of him.

One picture I have is of him fighting with my mother over money all the time. He was a heavy smoker—four packs a day—and here they were fighting about getting bread or getting milk, and he's pumping money into his lungs. I thought that was wrong. I had real mixed feelings about my father.

When I was very young, probably around three, my family moved from Coney Island to Brownsville. Brownsville, at that time, was a very large

Jewish neighborhood in Brooklyn. We lived on the third floor of a three-story brick building.

By and large, I enjoyed growing up there, had a lot of friends. It was pretty much the United Nations. Most of the kids, like myself, were Jewish, but their backgrounds were different—they were from Russian or German families. After a while, we had some Puerto Rican kids and black kids, and we had Italian friends on the block, too. So it was just a big mixture.

It was an interesting street. There was one block between my house and the elementary school we attended that was just industrial. On the corner, there was this rag factory. They had these huge bales of rags there, and they had this weird, musty odor, like somebody's stuff that's been in an attic too long.

On the corner across the street from that, there was this soda-bottling factory, and then, in the middle of the block, there was what we called a pickle factory. They had these huge barrels outside with these kosher pickles. So the route to school, all of a sudden, had this sort of pungent, musty odor from the rags. Then you'd get a little farther down the block, and you could smell the brine from the pickles.

Half a block from this street I'm describing, there was a huge industrial-size bakery that made rolls and French bread. I mean, you could sit on the roof of my house, and you'd have this just beautiful smell of warm bread baking over the whole neighborhood.

So you had this conglomeration of fragrances from the rags, and the pickles, and the dust of Brooklyn, and fresh bread. And somehow it all came together, and, at least in retrospect, it's ambrosia.

One of the things that impressed me after I got older was to realize our year had been governed by a religious calendar. For example, there was Succot, the harvest festival. The Orthodox Jews would build these houses out of bamboo or reeds, anything like that, in the yard. And they would have wine, and they'd have some sort of a celebration—I never could figure the whole thing out. But it was always a festive occasion, and it gave you a nice feeling.

And Simchat Torah, when the Spanish Jews I grew up with would carry the Torah through the aisles in the synagogue, with the people singing, then dancing a little bit. It was a nice time. And then we'd go from that to Hanukkah, which was fun, and from that a few months later to Purim in February or something like that.

Anyway, that was pretty much my world. And throughout that period, I really hadn't experienced anything like the anti-Semitism a lot of people talked about and which I discovered later on.

I had three brothers who were much older. Harry is the only one of my brothers I get along with real well. He's eight years older than I am. He was interested in music, and he used to listen to the Toscanini broadcasts all the time. It must have been during the forties and fifties.

Harry went into the service and left his record collection at home. I wasn't supposed to, but I started listening to them. I also liked to conduct—it was a power trip, I think. I took the chairs out of the kitchen and put them in this tiny bedroom. Then I'd crank Beethoven's "Ninth," and I knew the music well enough so that...I mean, it's great if you can go like *that* [gestures like a conductor] when the brass comes in. I still conduct while I'm driving in my car. It drives my wife crazy. She thinks I'll get into an accident.

When I was a kid, my brother Harry took me to see *South Pacific*, and I was blown away by it. I mean, it was just beautiful. Then we would go, occasionally, to concerts uptown. It was a long ride on the subway from where we lived in Brooklyn, and it would be a hell of a night. We would always sing along with the last number, "It's a Grand Night for Singing." We had a great time.

Harry took me lots of places; he even organized a backpacking trip once for the Boy Scouts and took me along.

We moved to Massachusetts when I was about fourteen, and suddenly I was a minority. I think there were three Jewish kids out of the entire population. I was like a fish out of water. People were talking about Jesus and the Virgin Mary and everything as though all this was obvious and everybody believed it. It really was a culture shock. I mean, I didn't know what to make of it. It was the first time in my life I remember somebody asking me, "Are you Catholic?" or "What are you?" and I found myself hesitating about what to say. And that had never happened to me before in my life.

I had a friend, Charles, who was my homeroom teacher in high school. We got into these occasional bull sessions. Anyway, that led to a friendship that actually continued until he died and I was married and had kids.

I guess I've made a career of getting a free education from people. I mean, it's not intentional on my part. Charles was a very important part of that free education because it was clear that I wasn't going anyplace in terms of college or anything like that. I read a lot, but I didn't know what the hell to read. I felt like he was one of several people who gave me, if not a free education, at least some help in disciplining my mind in a way that wasn't going to happen otherwise.

When I was fifteen, my sister-in-law, who was married to my oldest brother, introduced me to my wife. She didn't live too far from where I did, and so we started walking to school together. I'd meet her at her locker, and we'd walk around the school and all that stuff. You know. And we'd go to the sock hop and ... I really loved her. I was just blown away.

I think one of the things that appealed both to her and to me was how different we both were. She had grown up in this blue-collar family. I mean, they were as Catholic as you can get. The Infant of Prague was everyplace in that house. There were statues all over. Her family were dyed-in-the-wool anti-Semites. And for her to suddenly be going out with one of *them*. It was great.

We had lots of good times not doing anything in particular except going for a cup of coffee and smoking Lucky Strikes, going to an occasional movie.

When I went into the Navy after high school, we decided to elope. On one of my leaves, we went to New York and got married by a judge. We were both nineteen, so we were very young. We went back to Massachusetts, and, a few days later, we went to this Slovak church. There was a young priest there, and he did his number in the rectory. The ceremony had to be in the rectory because you couldn't have a Jew married inside the church.

After we got married, we basically went on our own. I think it was much harder for her than it was for me because she was closer to her family. She wanted their acceptance, and I think that they looked at her as a real screwball for actually going out and marrying a Jew. There were people in my family who felt the same way.

When I came out of the Navy, I needed a job right away because, by then, we had a baby and no money. I got it into my head I wanted to go to work for a newspaper. I went down to the newspaper in our hometown in Massachusetts, and I told the managing editor I was willing to start at the bottom. I said, "I have published some poetry, and I got real good marks in school on my essays." Most editors nowadays would just laugh you into the ground.

But this guy, even though later I came to regard him as an asshole, was very generous with me. He gave me a job for $65 a week and told me

I could write obits. I didn't even know how to do that, but there were these old guys around the office—probably the age I am now—who I was just incredibly impressed with because the city editor would come over and say, "Bill, give me a story on blah, blah, blah," and the guy would throw a piece of paper in the typewriter, and he'd just start writing it. I thought this was magic.

So I started watching these guys. Also, I would read *The New York Times* and *The Herald Tribune* as much as possible, and I just learned from mimicking the styles of other writers. I got very good at it.

I stayed there for two years, and then I got a job with UPI. And that was a whole new thing because I was not used to writing under the kind of pressure that you have at UPI, where everything is very, very fast. But I just kept asking questions and imitating, and so I got better and better at what I was doing. I have never been intimidated by my own ignorance.

This was the late sixties when this real heavy-duty idealism was rampant. My wife and I were involved in all the social movements and demonstrations, and we were kind of burned out. We had our kids in some little Marxist school—typical late-sixties nonsense. But at the same time, I had a full-time job and I was covering politics. I was doing more and more muckraking. It got to the point where I was getting a little paranoid about what I was doing because I was stepping on a lot of toes.

I have always liked to hike or backpack. Eventually, I decided I wanted to live where there were more places to do that. So my wife and I started talking about moving someplace west of the Mississippi. We both basically lived within a 200-mile radius of where we were born, and we didn't know anything about anyplace else.

There's a trade magazine called *Editor and Publisher* where all the newspapers in the country advertise for help. I saw an ad for a newspaper in Colorado. I remember saying to my wife, "Well, what can you lose? It's an eight-cent stamp." They interviewed me on the phone and asked me if I wanted to come out for an interview. They paid the freight, so I came out. And I loved it instantly.

You can imagine. I had never been out of the Northeast, and, all of a sudden, I'm here. I saw these mountains and the clear blue sky and all that, and I thought, "Good heavens!" I mean, it was just magic. I came, and I stayed with that paper for four years. After that, I was hired by another paper, and I stayed there for the next fifteen years.

I've gone through a lot of changes since I've been out here. For one thing, while I'm by no means a practicing Jew—I've gotten a million miles away from that—I'm very proud of the fact that I'm part of a tradition that has survived five or six thousand years. I think the tradition is beautiful, and I'm very happy about having that Jewish background, and specifically a Sephardic Jewish background. I don't want to lose that.

On the other hand, I can't see myself as somebody who goes to a synagogue every Saturday. I'm just basically not a joiner. What I prefer to do is create my religion as I go along, on a day-to-day basis. I know what the foundation of it is, but I don't feel like I want to impose that on anybody, and I don't want anybody to impose anything on me.

Every year, I observe Hanukkah at our house. I light the menorah, and my kids come over, and my grandchildren come over, and it's very nice. They all participate. At one time, I stopped doing that for a few years because I felt a certain hypocrisy. I was observing some religious holidays and not others. Then, suddenly, there came a time when I said, "Well, that's bullshit. I'll do what I feel comfortable doing and create my own definitions."

I've only come to this decision within the last ten years. What happened was that my wife and I were separated for a couple of years—about twelve years ago. I had gone through this crazy catharsis where I was trying to sort my feelings out, writing them down, trying to keep track of how I was feeling. My head was very, very screwed up.

There was complete chaos around that time. I was unhappy about a lot of the small things. The house was always a wreck. My wife was always busy and preoccupied with something or other. The kids were young, very demanding. I was under financial pressure. There was a whole bunch of stuff, all at the same time. I guess I was just feeling boxed in, with no way out, you know? I wasn't a happy camper.

I didn't think my wife had any more love or affection for me. We were maintaining the status quo. It was pretty clear from what was going on that I was just basically a stable element in the equation. I was here and she was here, and it's like we were both pretty much committed to the idea of marriage, so we stuck with it. But I had no idea anymore what it could feel like to really love someone and be loved by someone. It was just work, come home and get through the day, and that was it.

I was around forty when I had a serious affair with a younger woman. Although I hadn't been perfect in that respect over the course of my married life, I'd never actually felt like I'd fallen in love with somebody until this affair happened. I left my wife. I'd always had a close relationship with my kids, and I felt now like I couldn't face them. I'd disrupted everything. On the other hand, I felt like I had to do that because I was so emotionally involved with this woman; to stay home would be some kind of a fraud.

I really got emotionally involved, to the extent that I became the quintessential caricature of the middle-aged man who takes a tumble for a twenty-eight-year-old woman. I finally came to the conclusion that what I was doing was very self-indulgent. It was not really satisfying. It had no meaning. And it was out of character, so to speak.

At first, I didn't see it that way, but eventually I realized that the affair was really absurd. It was a very tempestuous period in my life, and, emotionally, I was a wreck. The thing that amazes me is that I was able to work. I still, to this day, don't know how I kept my job during that time.

The affair went on for about two years. The turning point came right around the time my wife and I were deciding whether or not we were going to get back together again. My father-in-law died. She was going back to Massachusetts, to the funeral, and she asked me to go with her. Because she was really upset. She was really close to her father. I felt a little funny about it, but I went.

I was in the church with her family. We were all sitting together, and they were having this funeral mass. I just was sort of looking around at all of her brothers and sisters and nieces and nephews. What struck me was that I was an integral part of that family. My wife and I had met when I was fifteen, so I had grown up with her brothers and sisters. I know them as well as I know anybody in my own family. And even though we have different viewpoints, and some of them are crazy, still, we are one unit.

And so we're sitting there in the pew in this church, and I'm thinking what I'm doing back in Colorado is crazy. It just doesn't fit. It was kind of a bittersweet feeling because, in a way, it was like seeing myself in a circle that had closed. On the one hand, it was a good feeling because I felt that I had discovered a context that I was a part of, that I belonged to, and that was somehow comforting.

But simultaneously, I looked around me, and it was really a narrow world and, in some ways, a dull world. And I wasn't sure that it was really what I wanted to be a part of. I kept vacillating and thinking, "Well, maybe it's not necessarily what I want, but this is the reality. I've been around these people since I was a kid. Our lives are linked. We know each other inside and out, and it's clear to me that they would be here for me, and obviously I would be here for them. This is my world. The rest may be a romantic fantasy."

So I realized, for better or worse, this is where I am, and I should accept that and try to build on it instead of trying to destroy it. Because even though there were some negative aspects to the marriage, there was a lot about it that was good and supportive.

After that, we decided to get back together and try to rebuild our marriage. It was very difficult at first. We were both very wary and somewhat distrustful. There was a period of redefinition. I had given a lot of thought to what was bothering me, to what I could and could not put up with.

Money, as you know, in any marriage is a big deal. I realized, for example, that I did not want to walk around broke all the time. I was working my ass off and just basically paying the bills, and half the time if I wanted to go out to lunch, I had to check to see if I had enough money. And I thought, that's ridiculous. I make half-way decent money. It shouldn't be that way.

So I insisted that a portion of my pay go into a separate checking account. And I told my wife, "You ought to do the same thing." So that was one of the changes—changing our attitude toward money.

We also started putting more time into planning vacations and little outings. We saw the necessity of getting away from the house, even if it was only to go to the movies more often and not be constantly preoccupied with domestic stuff like taking out the garbage.

Then, two-and-a-half years ago, I quit my job. What happened was, I got squeezed out. It was very typical of what was going on with guys my age all over the country. The paper just made life more and more miserable. I was making good money, and they kept upping the ante.

They started setting quotas. They wouldn't judge your performance on the basis of what kind of stories you were doing or how much work was involved. They'd say, "We need three dailies during the week," meaning three stories, "and a weekender," meaning a Sunday story. Essentially, what they were doing, which was unheard of when I started in the newspaper business, was to divide my salary by how many stories I wrote to determine how much each story cost them. It was never made quite that explicit, but that's what was going on.

They knew the one thing that I would not do was move, because I'm emotionally and economically invested in this community. This is where all my friends are and my kids and whatnot. Two-and-a-half years ago, they said,

"We're closing the branch office, and we really need you here to work on the city desk. We need you on re-write." Re-write on that paper is the kiss of death. Re-write is here, the door is there. Everybody knows that.

I'm not alone in being forced out of a job. There are literally millions of guys in my age group who have gotten squeezed out of jobs just at a point when they were going to become their most productive. Heading for the biggest bucks and the best jobs, they were put out on ice.

I was fifty when I quit. I was scared, and I wasn't scared. In retrospect, I'm really glad that I did it, because I didn't realize just how sick I was. I was real sick. In the last three years I worked for that place, I had undergone a personality change. I was under extreme pressure all the time. They would think nothing of sending me 150 miles away, then, before I'd had time to get any sleep, send me 200 miles in the other direction for another story. I was in knots all the time.

I wasn't living at all. I found it very, very hard to relax. I was angry most of the time. Some nights I'd come back from my office and start pounding the kitchen counter and calling these people I was working for every name under the sun. They were running me into the ground, and I hated it. I hated myself for putting up with it. I hated myself for lacking the courage to tell them to go to hell. I felt miserable. I felt trapped.

But it was scary because I had no savings, and the only thing that I had going for me at all was that, for several years while I was working full-time, I had continued to freelance. I wasn't making a lot of money freelancing, maybe seven or eight thousand bucks a year or less. But I always kept my hand in.

I remember toward the end, when things were getting real dicey at the paper, I thought maybe I should stop the freelancing. But I said to myself, "These people are trying to get rid of me. I'm going to have to have something to fall back on." I'm glad I didn't burn my bridges because, when I left there, I had $18,000 in freelance assignments under contract. Eighteen thousand bucks is not a tremendous amount of money, but, for a guy who is essentially unemployed, it felt okay. I was able to build on that. And I've done all right since.

During those last few years at the paper, I was constantly preoccupied with what someone else was thinking. What this one wanted me to do. What he was going to think of the product that I'd just turned in. Whether it was going to run on page one. What the reaction would be and how it would affect my future.

It was a totally consuming preoccupation. Afterwards I didn't have that. I didn't have to think about that at all. My time is my own right now. I juggle my schedule so that, if my granddaughter is having some sort of award ceremony at school, and somebody calls and says they want to get together for an interview, I say, "I can't do that. I've got a personal commitment." So I can take care of the things I consider important. I set my own priorities.

Six months after I left, people said, "Your face looks completely different. You look like a different person." I think that was a reflection of the fact that I had relaxed a lot. I had started paying attention to things I enjoy.

I like opera, so I subscribed to a magazine called *Opera Quarterly*. It costs fifty bucks a year, but I'm so interested in it. I started spending more time reading about opera, and I started spending more time listening to opera. I've always done that, but when I was under a lot of pressure, it was very hard to sit down in the living room and put on some earphones and dedicate that time. The wheels would always be spinning. I was basically a crazy man.

I started spending a lot more time with my kids and a lot more time tending to small things around the house. I got a better bike and took more bike rides. Started swimming more. I just relaxed. I also spent more time trying to define what was important to me.

The last two-and-a-half years have been an interesting time for me because I've had to redefine wealth for myself. When I left my job, I took a fifty percent drop in pay. I had convinced myself that I couldn't survive on less money. But what I found is that, if you have to, you can survive on less.

I'm surprised that I was able to survive. I was surprised at the kindness of some of my friends in the business. There were editors who would call and give me assignments, or talk to me about different projects I could work on. I had friends who were very supportive. I got by.

Just the experience of being able to work without this massive pressure on me all the time is so freeing. I've put a lot of time into a story I've been working on recently. And maybe I won't make an enormous profit on this story, but it's a satisfying experience. I'm enjoying all the people I'm talking to and all the research I'm doing. I'm enjoying the process of writing it, and it will appear in a very nice magazine.

Even when I think another assignment is never going to come through, something happens. But still, you don't know. Right now, I have enough work to keep me going through June. I don't know what the hell's going to happen after June. All I can do is look backwards and say, "Well, I've been there before." Something surfaces.

I think something happens, at least for someone like myself, as you get older. I was much more driven when I was younger. I would do anything for a story. Anything. I'd go any place, stay up for two days and go into an area where there were violent riots. I was driven. I wanted that kind of success. Now I feel much more at ease. If someone were to say to me, "Wouldn't you like to go to Bosnia and cover that civil war?" I'd say, "Go fly a kite." Give me a quiet mountaintop and an open can of beer. I'll be happy as anything.

But I think it takes a while to get to that point. It took a while to realize that people were paying me more money, not because they liked my face, but because they liked my performance. Over time, if you can just get enough of that, it helps to build your self-confidence. I suppose it's just a question of maturing and getting a lot of reinforcement.

I also think you become more acutely aware of what you care about and what you don't care about. And your values become more defined. I have a half-way decent house. It's no mansion. It's comfortable. I like the place, and I like the area where I'm living. I have a modest income, and my wife has a modest income. We are never going to be multimillionaires.

I'm just not that ambitious. There are people who will work twelve and eighteen hours a day to amass a fortune. I am not one of them. I don't give a shit about stuff like that. If I can meet my bills and keep the wolf away from the door, have a nice vacation occasionally, and have a tranquil relationship with my family, that's as good as it gets.

It's a lot better than it was twelve years ago when I was going nuts. But I don't know that you can be where I am when you're in your twenties. I think you have to be scorched a few times and sort it all out somehow.

I'm comfortable with the fact that at least I have a certain amount of security, good health, a decent family life, and I'm getting by. That is a quantum leap from where I started out. In my world, I've been successful. So, there it is.

Father Figures

Frank DeMaria

> I was always striving to get my father's approval, so I was always doing more and more and more to get his attention. Now I get my own satisfaction from achieving something in itself, even though I never got his approval. I'm not analytical enough to understand how I learned this. I guess I've learned it by accident...

We meet Frank DeMaria, a forty-nine-year-old architect, in his office late one summer afternoon. Sun comes in from the windows, falling on a large drafting table covered with drawings, pencils, and a draftman's parallel bar. Rolls of other plans are piled on the wooden desk. Various framed photographs of his three sons, marking their progress from birth, cover one wall.

Frank is about five-foot-seven with a slight frame. He wears a red plaid shirt and khaki chinos. His piercing black eyes are framed by full, arched eyebrows. As we talk, he occasionally rakes his graying beard with his fingers.

The grandson of Italian immigrants, Frank grew up with a strong sense of his heritage, especially its emphasis on family. His life has two important emotional markers that influence his identity at midlife—the father who abused him physically and psychologically as he was growing up, and the three sons he is now raising with love and pride.

Significant experiences in Frank's adult life—serving in Vietnam in his twenties, getting a degree in architecture in his early thirties, and suing for custody of his oldest child in his late thirties—continually forced him to discover his strengths and abilities.

In his forties, Frank has taken on new ventures, starting both a second business and a second family. His challenge as a professional has been to stop looking over his shoulder for his father's approval and to look to himself for validation of his work. With each success, he has become more sure of his architectural expertise.

Frank's young sons compete with his business for his time and energy. Remembering his own childhood, however, he is developing an affectionate, supportive bond with his children. He is clearly coming into his own in midlife and is building a self-image colored with pride, professional creativity, close family relationships, and a new appreciation of his ethnic roots.

I was born on November 25, 1943—that was Thanksgiving day during the war. I was born in Philadelphia, and I'm of one-hundred-percent Italian descent.

I grew up in a very male-dominated family, a very ethnic family. It instilled in the males, at least, a sense of pride, a sense of roots, a sense of respect for adults. The moral values were there. It was also a religious experience because, being Italian, we were also Roman Catholic. My life as a child was very much tied to the church as an altar boy and a choirboy.

As a child, I can remember going to my mom's parents' house all the time, with the males gathering in the dining room and the women and children gathering in the kitchen. My grandparents on both sides gave me love and attention, even though I didn't understand them half the time because they didn't speak English very well.

I can remember my cousin, who was about my age, and me sitting on the back porch with a coffee can full of corncob pipes that belonged to my grandfather, pretending we were smoking pipes, pretending we were my grandfather talking in Italian. Of course, neither of us knew what the hell he was talking about, or what the other was talking about. But we would sit on the porch and converse, with our hands flailing in the air. I have fun recalling childhood memories like that.

What wasn't fun was constantly getting my ass beat by my father, the failure of my father to understand that everything he did I didn't necessarily want to do, and everything he was I didn't necessarily want to be. My dad didn't have any patience with me. I always viewed myself as a very fun-loving kid, a clown, always wanting to have a good time. And my father didn't know what it was to laugh. He didn't know what it was to have a good time.

I never got any praise from my father, so, as a child, I was constantly striving for his attention or his approval. At almost fifty years old, I have yet to get his approval for anything. That instilled some incentive and some drive in me.

My mother's second oldest brother, my Uncle Rocco, had a farm, and, no matter what, he took the time and the patience to deal with me. I can always remember him defending me when my dad would get mad at me. I always remember him trying to teach me things around the farm, like how to sharpen a knife or how to plant a tomato. Giving me a sense of responsibility. Nothing astronomical, but the man gave me a sense of importance. And the neatest part was, when I did something right, he praised me for it.

The older I got, the more difficult it became to deal with my dad. He expected more, and I got less. The last time that bastard hit me I was eighteen years old. I had a girl I was dating with me, and he didn't like the idea of me coming home to his house with a girl, and he said something to me. I don't remember what it was. Then he just hauled off and decked me. That was the last time I remember him hitting me—that's not the last time he tried, but it was the last time he did it.

I guess in high school I was what today would be called a "nerd." I didn't know how to socialize with people. I went to high school with kids I had known from kindergarten. We grew apart because I didn't grow with them physically. I was a runt. The guys I knew as a little kid had become Mr. Football, Mr. Basketball, Mr. Baseball. I wasn't Joe Jockstrap. I was Joe Dingleberry, somewhere in the background.

I went to college to become an engineer, a civil engineer because my father was a civil engineer, and that's what he wanted me to do. I was rebellious, and I flunked out at the end of the first year. I went to a drafting school, a kind of junior college, and I learned how to be a draftsman.

I lived with some friends. I feel like I started my socialization process at eighteen instead of eight. I had a lot of maturing to do. I was eighteen and didn't know how to pay bills or balance a checkbook. I didn't even know what the hell a checkbook was.

I had to learn with four other people in the same small area. I had to share dishes with four people who had different attitudes about what and how they ate, four different attitudes about everything. I lived with those guys until I was about twenty-four. I was in the Navy Reserves, and then I had to fulfill my active duty, so I went to Vietnam.

I wasn't afraid of the war, but I hated to leave my job and my friends. My life had started to settle down a little bit. I had made a good friend, actually, whose name was John Schmidt. We started riding motorcycles together. John taught me all about "pussy." I first found out what it was all about on the night of my twenty-first birthday. That was the night I got laid for the very first time. I was so drunk I don't remember it.

I remember going to the bus station to leave town to report for duty. My mom was there, but my dad wasn't there, and neither were my two sisters.

But my friends had taken me to the bus station and were there to bid me a fond farewell.

Mail call in Vietnam was something everyone looked forward to. You'd have to have been there to understand what it was like to be the only one who didn't get any mail. I never got a letter from my mother or my father. I never got a thing from my two sisters.

It was embarrassing. It was demoralizing. I really didn't give a fuck if I came home or not. That's why I extended my stay to over eighteen months.

The hardest part of Vietnam for me was my family, their lack of support. I got shot in the back. A mortar round blew up behind me and tore the living shit out of me. It tore my right ear off and messed up my face. I was quarantined for a long time because I had so many infections. I hadn't even listed my family as next of kin—I listed my best friend as next of kin. To this day, my family doesn't know I got wounded.

When I got back, I tried to find out who I was. I found out I wasn't a very happy person. I sat on the front porch with my mother one day after I had knocked her on her ass when she grabbed me one morning to wake me up. By instinct, I had decked her. Anyhow, she said, "You were a happy person when you left, but you're not a happy person now." My family never understood what it was they did to me, let alone what Vietnam did to me.

About Vietnam—I don't regret what I did, and I'd do it again if I had to. I felt a sense of patriotism. I think that comes from being Italian-American. More accurately, I had a sense of responsibility. I was allowed to live in this country, and I felt an obligation to repay it.

I got a job in an architectural firm after I got back. I was given more responsibility than I'd ever had in my life. I was in charge of construction of a historical center. I've always had a third dimension in the back of my head about why things go the way they go—construction, mechanical things—and I picked that job up real quickly. There were maybe two hundred people working under my supervision on that job. I had to earn their respect. Once I learned the job, they accepted me.

But when I was with the educated groups, the honchos in the office, they looked down at me because I was one of the "baby killers." To them, I was a warmonger, a rapist, and a pillager. I stayed away from those types as much as possible. They always asked stupid questions like "Did you kill anybody in Vietnam?"

I wanted to associate with educated people, but educated people didn't want to associate with me. An architect I worked with told me my problem was credibility, because I didn't have a degree. That pissed me off, and I made up my mind I was going back to college.

It took me five years after I got home to get back in college. Some administrator told me to my face that, because I was Italian and a veteran, I would never make it through college. Well, I earned my way through school. I worked my ass off and got two scholarships. And I had some money from the federal government because of Vietnam.

I went back into architecture. If you ignored the first year I fucked up in school, you'd find I graduated third in my class of 175. I was in my early thirties by then, and the kids called me "Grandpa" or "The Old Man." Some of them treated me differently because I was a veteran.

I don't know why I wanted to be an architect. Partly to piss my old man off, partly because it was creative. I had worked in the engineering profession for five years. An engineer does the same thing day after day after day. An architect creates environments for other people. I build homes for people now. I leave an impression that lasts in what I build. I create with my head and my hands, and I leave things that people will always remember.

In less than a year after I graduated, I sat for my state boards, which is something you generally don't get to do in architecture until six years after you graduate after college. Still, I couldn't get a job—or rather, the only one I could find paid just $8,000 a year.

I said the hell with that. I started my own little company. I did construction work on people's houses while continuing to do architecture, design, on the side. I was happy. I was able to work with both my head and my hands.

I got married a couple years out of college to someone I had been living with. When we were dating, we did a lot of different things together. We went hunting, camping, fishing. I had a good time. When I was getting ready to graduate, she put me in a box. She said we had to get married or she would leave.

I let her leave, but it tore me up. I was torn up over the emotional need to have someone around. I'm not telling you that I was in love—it was just a need for someone to physically be there for a change.

I got so involved in that emotional need that I couldn't concentrate on my education. So I agreed to get engaged. I went ahead and got married, I guess, because here I was thirty-two years old, and I was feeling the peer pressure. It wasn't okay just to hang around with the guys so much. People, my family especially, began to wonder if I wasn't gay.

My wife and I constantly argued about sex. About money, too. Then she got pregnant without anything resolved between us, really. We went to a marriage counselor, but the marriage didn't last.

I was thirty-seven when I got divorced. That's when I hit a real low point in my life—in a business sense and on a personal level. My wife's attorney tied up my bank account and my business. I couldn't enter into contracts. At the time, I had over a million dollars of business under contract, and I had to give it all away.

I wasn't allowed to take anything out of the house, and my business was located in my house. The only things I could take out were my personal possessions, which were generally defined as what I could put on my back. Eventually, I just gave up and went to work for a firm of architects and engineers.

My whole family stayed away from me. They were embarrassed by the divorce. They didn't want to get close to my son either, because they said they wouldn't see him much since my wife would have custody. The baby was eighteen months old when we got divorced. I immediately started a custody battle. The most rewarding time of my day had been coming home and hearing that kid calling for me. He'd always come running to me when I hit the door.

Everywhere I went, I was admonished for fighting for my son, because men are not supposed to get the kids. I even got flak from my friends, even from one who was a minister. They all said I was doing a bad thing by trying to take my son away from his mother.

As to the custody battle, I had to fight for what I believed in—but I was the only one who believed in it. Everybody thought I was wrong. I had no place to go, no one to talk to.

I became more and more bitter because, as a man, I was supposed to have control over my life. And I *did* have control, before the divorce. I controlled what I ate, slept, and wore. I controlled where I worked. When I got divorced, I couldn't even control my bowel movements anymore.

As a male, I was always taught to be macho, not to cry. My divorce taught me how to cry. I cried for hours, day after day, to the point where there were no tears left. I couldn't eat, and I lost a lot of weight. I cried for the loss of my child more than anything else. And for the fact that I was alone. I had no one. I fought for custody of my son for nine years. That was a terrible experience.

I had been stripped of dignity. I didn't have any money or friends. People looked at me as unstable, irrational. How alone can you get? I was in Vietnam, and I was never as alone there as I was when I went through that divorce. I probably spent the same amount of time getting the divorce as I did in Vietnam, and I could do Vietnam again on my head in comparison to that divorce.

It really affected my health. I got to the point where I would shake so badly I scared myself. I lost so much of my hair. Because my wife filed for the divorce originally, I was always the defendant, even in the custody battle. I was always having to defend myself.

Every dime I made—my taxes, everything—was scrutinized by somebody else. Every time I was hauled into court, they wanted to know what I had bought the last time I had gone to the grocery store, how much money I had spent on myself. It was hard to get up and go to work some days. Everything seemed like punishment, punishment, punishment. It was like being in jail.

I joined Fathers For Equal Justice, a support group. I even became president. When I first got involved with the group, it was for support. But after a while, it was like a wound that you constantly poured salt into. I couldn't get over my bitterness because I was surrounded by it all the time.

I also joined a Catholic singles group. I'd hear women talk about "that no good son-of-a-bitch," and all of a sudden, I realized that *I* was that no good son-of-a-bitch. I was sure that was what my wife was saying to people.

Because of these groups, I just couldn't seem to put the hatchet away. I was bitter. I couldn't seem to relate to anyone for any extended time. I guess I was depressed. My boy would cry when I had to take him home on Sunday. It got so he wouldn't eat on Sunday night because he knew that after dinner he'd be going home. When crying didn't work, he started hiding in my apartment.

I remember one day, taking him home, I was going around a corner past this building and he started crying. I pulled over and asked him why he was crying, and he said, "Because you don't love me anymore." I said, "What do you mean?" And he said, "You went past that building and you didn't say you loved me."

I always took the same route home, and apparently I had set a pattern of telling him I loved him when we went past this building. He had gotten it so entrenched in his head, that building and me loving him. After that, I'd take a different route every time I took him home. Things like that tore me up. I called that boy every day for nine years.

The continuing experience in court suing for custody of my son was dreadful. It was nine years and $40,000 worth of shit. My son asked me just recently if I would do it again. I would.

I dated my present wife for five or six years before we got married, and, about a year after we were married, we began to have some problems. It was about the time my mother fell into a coma, and once again tremendous feelings of loss and loneliness crept up on me. I cried and cried during this time. A week after my mother died, my wife and I went to a marriage counselor.

I'm still with my wife. We've worked things out. She's a solid woman, a good person. And now we have two little boys.

Anyway, now I wanted something for myself again. I started back in business for myself, as an architect and builder, when I was forty-seven, two years ago. But in my profession, if you haven't arrived where you need to be by age thirty-two, you're generally considered burned out, useless. That's just a fact of life because the profession puts such a high demand on your talents. I didn't graduate from college until I was thirty-five, so where the hell was I? I was already in a hole.

My life crisis was getting my son back. It took a lot of my time and energy, for years. When I got him, it took a big burden off me, and it probably let me put my energy into my professional stuff. Professionally, I'm supposed to be dead at age fifty. I'm supposed to be sitting back administrating for some company. But I'm just getting started.

I'm forty-nine now, and I still have a lot of creativity and a lot of drive. When I solve a problem or design a house, it's like eating a good steak—it's really filling. It's the same feeling you have when you sit down with a good steak, a good cigar, and a Drambuie. That's the best way I can describe it. It's filling.

I don't know where I get the energy to handle the work and the kids. You know, it's instinct when you've been hit as a kid to hit your own kids, boot them in the butt. But I've kept saying to myself, "There's got to be a better way." Sure, I want my kids to obey, not to be unruly. I tell them they need to obey my rules in my house. But whipping doesn't do any good. I have flashbacks to my childhood, and I understand that.

I may spank these kids, but I don't whale on them. And when I do spank them, I catch myself because I don't want to fly off the handle and treat them the way my dad treated me. I love my three boys. I feel bad that I don't have enough time to spend with them.

Joe came to live with me when he turned eleven. I take him to work with me now that it's summer. I'm putting a toolbox together with him. I try to teach him things, things my dad never taught me. I give him duties and responsibilities in my office, and he seems to enjoy it. I compliment him when he does a good job, but I jump on him when he screws up, too.

Joe has some fear about our relationship. One day he asked me if our relationship would become like mine with my father. He and I fight sometimes, but we always kiss and make up. I always tell him I'm so proud of him. He's really my first love. We've fought a lot of battles together.

When I get up in the morning, the three-year-old says, "Daddy, give baby shower," so I take him in with me, even if I'm running late. The baby wakes up in the morning and just coos. He never cries. I like rocking him in the morning. Every night, I carry both the little ones up to bed on my back, which is half broken at my age. But I have to carry both up.

I tuck them in. If they cry in the middle of the night, I'm the one who gets up with them. I try to play with them. One of the bad parts of getting older is that you don't have the physical energy to keep up with little children. But we do play. And we spend a lot of time hugging and kissing.

My wife was concerned about my working so much, so she signed me up with the Italian-American club a couple of years ago. I got involved in it and stayed with it. These are people who were brought up in the same values and traditions I was brought up in—not necessarily like with my father, though.

I've met some really neat guys there. I'm probably close with about fifteen of them. When I'm with these guys, I feel better. I don't have to prove anything with them. For example, every Tuesday we have lunch, a group of us. Everybody's been divorced, everybody's got their aches and ailments, and we sit around and talk about this stuff.

This circle of friends has given me an outlet I never had before. They know where I come from ethnically. They understand me and my values. If I need a friend to talk to or help with something, I can call up one of these guys, no question. This has made a big change in my life. It has made me proud again of where I come from and who I am.

My past hasn't been too bright and rosy. I was always striving to get my father's approval, so I was always doing more and more and more to get his attention. Now I get my own satisfaction from achieving something, even though I never got his approval. I'm not analytical enough to understand how I learned this. I guess I've learned it by accident over a period of years.

Vietnam was probably the first time I thought about this stuff. You learn a lot sitting around in a foxhole while you're waiting to get your ass shot off. I've seen what I can create, but I've also seen what I can destroy. When you find out what you can create, that's what's important. That you can appreciate.

I'm almost fifty now, and I'm still trying to figure out how to deal with some problems, like how to handle arguments. I know I don't have to fight like I used to. But I don't have to eat crow, or pigeon, or anything else. I have some pride now.

I remember years back when I would get so frustrated I would go out and get shitfaced. When I woke up the next morning, I found out that not only did I still have the same frustration, but now I had a goddamn headache and a sore stomach to deal with. So I was only compounding my problems. Ignoring problems isn't the same as solving them. I'm still learning.

I'm working in the present, and I live for a better future. I'm creating that future now. I don't feel like I have any constraints in my life anymore. I can do what I want. I feel like I have finally come of age. I have a different set of values, based, basically, on my own approval of what I do with my family and my profession. Now I sit back and watch these values, or goals, grow. Just like I put money in a bank and watch to see if it grows interest.

I'm also trying to create an opportunity for my boys, if they want it, in my company. Joe likes the idea of "DeMaria and Sons." That excites him. I told him it would be "DeMaria Sons and Dad" because they can take over. I want my kids to have a good future. That's why I exist, and that's why I go on. I've had to create my own purpose, and they are it. In a sense, I'm growing up with my kids.

Celebrating Miracles

Jay Johnson

There comes a point in people's lives when they assess their situation, and they come to a real awareness that something has to change. I had met me, and I didn't like him, and I knew something had to change. But I guess my turnaround came consistent with not drinking and drugging, and with being okay with having my feelings.

In the '50s and '60s, rebellious behavior and drinking among adolescent boys often was not taken seriously. It was excused and dismissed with the phrase "Boys will be boys." For some boys, however, defiant behavior was not a harmless phase but a reaction to unexpressed feelings, or to restrictive social and institutional messages.

This was the situation for Jay Johnson, a Native American raised on the Indian Reservation in Cherokee, North Carolina. The death of his father when Jay was in his adolescence exacerbated an already-budding rebellious nature. His only models for dealing with loss were stoical ones.

Having no outlet for his grief, Jay turned to alcohol, which masked his feelings until he was well into his thirties. A turning point came when he met accepting people through human-relations training, people who granted him permission to grieve and to have his feelings. Gradually, he was able to come to terms with his alcohol addiction and to reassess his values.

Jay's change has helped make it possible for him to live out his dream of making a difference in the lives of others. His current work in a chemical-dependency treatment center for Native American adolescents allows the potential others have always recognized in him to become a reality.

We meet for breakfast on a warm spring Saturday at a popular local restaurant near Jay's home in Cherokee. Jay's Native American heritage is not immediately obvious in his appearance. His sandy-colored hair, pale blue eyes, and sprinkling of freckles hint at the possibility of an Irish influence in his background. His manner of speaking is a richly diverse mix. He manages to pack the wisdom of an elder, the orneriness of a good ol' boy, and the passion of a country preacher into a single voice.

We talk amid a background of breakfast conversations and the clatter of dishes. A waitress pours numerous cups of coffee as Jay tells his story.

I was born in Cherokee in 1947. My father was an enrolled member of the Eastern band of Cherokee Indians, and my mother was an enrolled member of the Western band.

A primary remembrance out of those earlier years is the summers, and I guess I still have a fondness for summers. I can remember days in the summertime that just … Lord, they went on forever! It seemed like you could live a lifetime in a day. Learning about bees and snakes and all kinds of boy things with my buddies. Playing on the river, catching fish, ball games.

We used to go down to the river every day, and there was a big tree there. Some of the older kids could climb that tree like a cat, and they'd drop out into the river. We always met about the same time down there, and one day I was there early, and I climbed the tree. I was just looking at the river and thinking, "God, that's a long way down," and I knew there was no way I was going down.

When I turned around, two other boys had showed up behind me saying it was my turn to jump. I said, "You guys go ahead and I'll climb back down." They said, "No. The rule is if you climb the tree you have to jump." I said, "I don't know how to swim." They said, "You didn't consider that when you climbed the tree." I didn't jump—I was pushed. That was the day I learned how to swim.

I guess that was also the day I learned that feelings never come in isolation. They always came in bunches. I was mad as hell at my buddies who pushed me, proud as punch I'd learned to swim, scared that it had actually happened. Just a whole gamut of "God, this is great" and "Oh shit" at the same time.

The first major change in my life happened when I was fifteen and Dad died. I learned that I could introduce stuff into my mouth—like liquor and beer—that made my mind feel different. It was a way to numb out and not feel. It worked real, real well. Real well.

I saw my mom take her faith and wrap it around her like she didn't have any feelings, like she was strong enough to walk through that. I got the message loud and clear that it wasn't okay to show my feelings.

I went to military school for a year before I went to college. It was my mom's last-ditch effort to teach me some discipline and respect. Military school is not the place to send folks who are estranged from their emotions and who know about alcohol. That's the last place you want to send any-body to teach them discipline and respect. Those things come out of a con-text of love and honesty. They're not found in a military institution.

That first summer after high school, I got a letter from the draft board. Vietnam was starting to perk. I went to the induction center, and this corporal came in the room, and he was what I've since come to call "Mickey Military" through and through. He took it real, real seriously. The first words out of his mouth were "Those of you who can read and write, stay where you are. Those who can't, move to the right-hand side of the room." And I thought, "Mister, this is 1966. Who the hell are you kidding?"

To my amazement, half the room got up and moved to the right. To my further amazement, most of the folks who sat still were sent home. Most of the folks who moved to the right stayed the night and caught the bus to basic-training camp. Those were the expendable ones.

That fall, I went off to college. I'm sure I had all the trimmings of country-come-to-town. Oh God! I can remember being real nervous. I had learned long ago about first impressions and how important they were. So when I walked up to the lady who was doing room assignments and she said, "Do you read?" I said, "Pardon me?" And she said, "Johnson?" I said, "Yes." "A.J.?" I said, "Yes." She said, "Do you read?" I said, "Pardon me?" She was getting a little more exasperated, and she said, "You read?" And I said, "Hell, yes, I can read." She said, "No, your dorm is 'New Reed'." I thought, "Aw, I'm dead." I had had that bad experience with those folks who got shipped to Vietnam because they couldn't read. Then I thought, "I can read! I've got the right answer!"

I got kicked out at end of the first year. The first semester I had a GPA of .067 or something like that. Like I said, I had understood about beer and liquor for several years. I did alcohol, and I stayed in my room a lot.

Obviously, they didn't recognize potential. Everybody had always told me that I had great potential. I've subsequently learned that great potential ain't worth a shit until it goes into action. So I went back to Cherokee and worked as a desk clerk at a motel.

In January, I went back to school. They put me on academic probation the first semester back. I learned to play bridge. Between bridge and Pabst Blue Ribbon, you can screw up a college career real quick.

It was still winter, and we had finished a bridge game in a dorm a quarter mile from my dorm. I had rolled down the steps, I recall, in my underwear.

I had made it outside the building and stopped to rest on my back in the snow, in the middle of a boxwood hedge. As only fate could have it, the director of admissions walked by and said, "What are you doing?" I said, as only a lovable drunk can say, "Counting the stars, sir." In about a foot of snow, in this boxwood, in my underwear. He said that he wanted to see me in his office in the morning. He advised me not to be late.

In his office that day, he told me that I was a clown, a nonconformist, and a country boy with that old I-don't-give-a-damn attitude. He said that I did not belong in college society. Well, I was eighteen years old and had been in dire pain for three years, probably as emotionally constipated as any human you've ever seen in your life.

By God, the admissions director had hit the nail on the head. Yes indeed, I was a clown. I loved to see people laugh and have a good time. Nonconformist? That, too. Because if nonconformist meant you thought for yourself then, yeah, I fit in that category. Because I had a head, and I knew how to think. "Country boy with that old I-don't-give-a-damn attitude?" You got it! I'm country, I'm a boy, and I don't give a damn. Didn't fit into college society? I *knew* I didn't belong there.

So as I packed my stuff that day to go back to Cherokee again, I made a decision that I was going to graduate from there if for no other reason than to give the place a bad name. The next semester I went back and made the dean's list just to show them I could. I didn't graduate from there, but I stayed long enough to build a grade-point average sufficient to transfer to Western Carolina University.

Then I got married. I had met my wife during my first year in college. We dated off and on for a couple of years, and in 1968 we got married and moved to Cherokee. I went to school, and she went to work. As long as I was in school, I had some money coming from Social Security because of my dad's death. So I had enough money to keep gas in an old car and drink a little beer on the weekends. Life was good. I declared a major in psychology. Finally, I was in a field that I really liked. I jumped into it in a big, big way.

In my junior year, I quit college and went to work for the police department in Cherokee. I had a new wife and a new baby. I was twenty-one years old, and they told me I was responsible, essentially, for defending the Constitution of the United States, as well as the state of North Carolina, God, motherhood, and apple pie, in that order. I strapped a .38 special around my leg and put a gold star on my chest.

It's real strange, the mentality you can develop from that kind of power. Nothing moved at night unless we said it was okay to move. Because we'd stop and challenge it. Anything we wanted to do, we did. Because of the great amounts of stress such responsibility created, we'd get off work, drink a six-pack, go home, and go to bed. You do that often enough, and you start looking for ways to create stress so you can drink the six-pack, go home, and go to bed. At any rate, my job at the police department didn't last long.

I went to work next as a teacher's aide in the high school. I worked with a math teacher teaching remedial math. After that year, I realized the difference between being a teacher's aide and being a teacher was about $400 per payday. So I said, "I'll go back to school."

At that time, our son was three and our daughter was three weeks old. My buddy came and asked if my wife and I would consider being house parents at the children's home. So they hired us. Work at the children's home paid for the rest of my college education.

During that time at the children's home, my life took a different direction. One of the men on the staff there was into some personal-growth training stuff, which I thought was the most ludicrous bunch of touchy-feely, gobbledy-goop bullshit that anybody had ever heard of in their life. Everybody knew that if you have emotions, you're supposed to suck 'em, swallow 'em, whatever you need to do with them, but you certainly didn't adhere to them, you certainly didn't listen to them, and God knows you didn't give in to them. You just acted as if you didn't have them. And that's really well put because we don't have them—they have us.

Anyway, I started going to these training events, and I met a bunch of people who were involved in personal growth. They weren't in test planes or anything, but they were certainly pushing the limits of the human condition, at least as far as I knew. Lots and lots of folks. I can't recall names, but I remember warm smiles telling me I was okay. There was nothing to prove. I didn't have to be anybody or do anything.

I had probably carried my dad around for twenty years, and I was tired. I was dog-ass tired of carrying a dead man around. But I couldn't find no place to lay him. I off-loaded him at one of those personal-growth labs. Or down-loaded him, anyway.

I talked about him, and cried about him, and grieved. I ranted and raved and raked God over the coals. I cursed God and maybe found God at the same time, I don't know, but it all seemed to fit together. I let my dad be dead, so I could get on with living. Twenty years was a long time to live as if things didn't hurt that really did hurt.

My life began to turn around after that. My search with my dad had been wanting to hear him tell me that he loved me. He would never be able to do that, and I became aware that without me being able to say that to me, nothing would matter. I had thought the love had to come from him. I learned that love isn't something you earn; it's something you accepted about yourself.

I think that was when the "shoulds" and the "oughts" in my life began to evaporate. One of my "shoulds" was about what nice guys do, how nice guys behave. Always try to do what's right, whatever the hell that is. Do the right things, say the right things, be nice—all the American Dream stuff. Go to church, work hard, save your money, and grow up to be president.

I think that was where my inhibition about anger came from. Good people didn't get angry. Once I had watched my father get explosively angry—I was fourteen at the time—and it had seemed like almost immediately following that one explosive incident he was stricken with cancer. Lying in the hospital, he just became wasted.

So my association with anger was death. If you got explosively angry or lost your cool, God would zap you. As a result, I knew great loads of fear. It seemed as though if I even breathed wrong, things might happen wrong. I think my freedom came with realizing there was no external source of power that needed to be tapped. The source was internal.

I graduated from college while I was working for the children's home. I went to work as director of an alcohol and mental-health program. Sometimes I would talk to the staff psychiatrist about the changes I was going through. One day he said, "You're obviously living by a set of values. What you need to do is go through them one at a time and see who they belong to." Over the period of the next several years, I did that.

Of course, I was still drinking. You can't work in that kind of job without building up great loads of stress and serious mental problems. And alcohol took the edge off. It helped me not to feel others' pain, or my own pain. It's a great anesthetic.

I had known that what needed to happen for folks wasn't happening the way we were going about it in the mental-health and alcohol program. There wasn't enough support. There wasn't enough continuity to it. So I started an AA group at Cherokee.

Until I sat and listened to a bunch of folks around the AA table, I'd never had permission to have a God of my own understanding. I had always had a God of everybody else's understanding. I needed one that I could put in my shirt pocket.

There comes a point in people's lives when they assess their situation, and they come to a real awareness that something has to change. I had met me, and I didn't like him, and I knew something had to change. But I guess my turnaround came consistent with not drinking and drugging, and with being okay about having my feelings.

Of all the addictions, alcohol is probably the most harmful because it's the most pronounced, and it impacts in a very visible way. Addiction is what drives a wedge between me and my power. The addiction can be a person, it can be a place, it can be a thing. But it's always something that disconnects me from me. And when I disconnect from me, I disconnect from power.

At this point in my life, I don't have to have an adrenaline rush. In fact, I hate adrenaline now. It always takes me off in a direction I don't want to go. I like real simple things at this point. Like my redheaded grandbaby. Lord God, what a trip! Absolutely has me wound around whatever way she wants me. She's probably three feet tall, forty pounds. I'm six-foot-five, 320 pounds, and she can twist me just like Play-doh. It just breaks my heart to watch her. And the other granddaughter, just the same way. God, those kids!

There's nothing in a drink of liquor or a hit of marijuana or anything else that has even come close to what goes off in my head and my heart about those kids. It's an out-of-body kind of experience. I've always prided myself on having a vocabulary, but I don't have words to describe this ...

I've had some miracles in my life. I heard a man on television the other day say, "Cancer has been real good for me." And the announcer said, "What do you mean?" And he said, "If you get to open your eyes and you're looking at your ceiling, it don't get no better than that." It doesn't happen for a lot of people. They don't get to wake up. So that's the first miracle.

The second one, there's a woman, my wife, who loves me in spite of my shit and in spite of my stupidity and my struggles, for all my insanity, for all my trying to run her off. She wouldn't run off. After doing every damn thing to prove to that woman that I was unlovable, she said, "Bullshit. You're lovable, and I'm gonna prove it." God gave her to me. Ain't no doubt in my mind how that worked out.

The third miracle, I know—a little bit—that I'm lovable. A little bit. There's still a real seedy character that lives in here, but there's a balance between the seedy character and the one that's lovable.

And the fourth miracle is what twelve-step folks call an "attitude of gratitude." Being thankful for all the stuff that's happened, because it took all of that—no matter how crappy, how terrible, how petty—to make the evolution. It's like the rose. There's thorns, and it doesn't grow without a lot of shit being piled around it. So it's just an attitude of being grateful for my life, grateful for the people who are in it.

And the fifth miracle is the most recent. I'm now working as a treatment-services supervisor at a regional youth-treatment center in Cherokee, a twenty-bed adolescent-treatment facility. We work with Native American youth between the ages of twelve and twenty-one.

Everything that happens in the youth-treatment center happens around the Medicine Wheel. The Medicine Wheel is a tradition that varies from tribe to tribe. What we try to do is present a generic version, so kids have something to grasp. The wheel relates to the four directions and the four colors, and we tie animal symbolism to those directions. Progression is measured around that wheel.

When folks first come to treatment, they're at an introductory level. They're not yet on the wheel, which is literally the wheel of life. They're at a coyote level. We challenge them first to explore what it feels like to be a coyote—to hunt by yourself, to be alone, to always be looking over your shoulder, to always be vigilant, to never have any rest, to always be moving, with nothing ever really stable. And we help them get in touch with those feelings, and that aloneness, and that powerlessness.

Then, once they've done that, we welcome them onto the wheel with a ceremony, to the introductory level of the deer. Learning to be gentle with yourself. Learning to be still, be cautious, but not quite as hyper-vigilant. And to begin to be around other folks of your own kind, to have some trails that are familiar, to walk periodically and build some pathways.

They progress from there into the wolf level, the level of the pack animal, and they learn the strength in that unity, where a number of folks who work alike make life a lot simpler. And they explore what those feelings are like.

Then we move to the bear clan. We don't actually call them clans, because some tribes are offended by that term. But it's about how bears do things. They innately know when it's time to do what they need to do, to take care of themselves and their young.

From there, we bring them to the last part, which is the eagle part. You know, eagles fly, but they never flock—and they mate forever. They're beautifully independent, functioning creatures that know how it all works.

I generally challenge the kids as they leave the program to be natives first. I say something like, "You may be the only native person some folks ever meet, and they're going to judge every one of us by how they see you. If you're drunk and lying in the ditch, they're going to assume that all Indians are drunk and lying in the ditch."

I'm real pleased with what we're doing. It's exciting to see folks change from looking down and feeling hopeless, to kind of taking life and shaking it. To see them picking their heads up and see their eyes develop some sparkle. To see them come alive.

When these kids go home, they have self-respect. They hold their heads up. They believe in themselves. There ain't nothing mystical or magical about what we do. We teach them that they're lovable. Lovable, valuable, and worthwhile.

I've changed. It used to be I couldn't sit in the same room with the up-line superiors at work who have something to say about my position or my ability, because I thought they were stuffed shirts. I thought they didn't know their ass from a hole in the ground. I thought they didn't care about people.

I've grown. I've learned I don't always have to be a hard-ass about things because I know better or believe differently. I can let people have their say. That's flexibility. Yeah, that fits for me. Now I can sit on the governing board and say what's appropriate.

So the most recent miracle is that I get to be in my dream. I get to share what I know with folks who seem to benefit from it. My life without service to others doesn't make any sense. Maybe that's something I learned early. Or maybe that's becoming aware of debts of gratitude—that, for whatever reason, I didn't die when I was twenty-one, even though I thought I was supposed to.

I'm also grateful that I got to hang around, and watch my kids grow up, and watch my grandkids. My father never lived to see his grandkids. Hell, he never lived to see me grow up. So just getting to watch this whole thing evolve into the second generation is mind-boggling for me.

As long as we stay asleep, we don't need answers. Only when we wake up. Life hurts too much when you try to stay numb, or when you have to pretend too much. When you give up the lie, then you get...I think scripture calls it a "peace that passes all understanding." It defies human understanding, the peace that comes.

By Myself

Fred Marshall

Being by myself is one of the greatest things that has happened to me. It's allowed me to know Fred. It's allowed
me to deal with my divorce. There's peace of mind there.
This may sound kind of selfish, but I like having that
space and not having to share it. I feel like, all my life, I've
been around people. I've never been alone. This is new.

*Fred Marshall, a forty-nine-year-old black portrait photographer, seizes on
an idea for the client with whom he is working and grins broadly. He gestures
excitedly and vaults across the studio to demonstrate the pose he has just
envisioned. His movement is, no doubt, a carry-over from his adolescence
when he ran track.*

*Fred is a self-described romantic who loves photographing weddings. His
shirt is starched and ironed to perfection, and his slender physique attests
to regular visits to the gym. Touches of grey in his hair and mustache are
his only concessions to age.*

*Watching Fred move around his studio, one imagines that his ideas have
a direct connection to his body. And although he is extremely animated,
Fred is not aggressive or intimidating. In fact, his clients easily recognize
him as a person of humor and goodwill. But his joy in living has been
informed by loss.*

*Fred was raised in an era of social stability by parents who instilled respect
for the wisdom of adults. When his parents insisted he marry his pregnant high
school sweetheart, he deferred to their advice. Fred's personal life for the next
two decades was profoundly affected by that decision. College and career
plans were eliminated from the picture and replaced with lessons about love
and survival that would support him through two major life crises. Then, in
his twenties, Fred's life was shattered by the death of his young wife, which left
him with two young children to raise alone. They were nearly grown when he
discovered he could earn a living from his much-loved hobby, photography.*

*Now, in midlife, following the collapse of a second marriage, he is
learning the value of being alone. Fred is finding unexpected pleasure in
being by himself and is developing a personal confidence he only previously*

experienced in his professional life. The course of Fred's life had required taking care of others first, now he is learning to nurture and care for himself.

My mother died in labor, having me. My aunt and uncle raised me. My aunt was my father's sister and couldn't have kids. My arrival was, I guess, a blessing to them. They had a son now. So that's how I was raised, and that's who I know as my mother and father. I had love there at that house.

The relationship with my real father...it wasn't very good. I don't know, it seemed like it was hard for him to show affection and love. I was always afraid to call him because he had this real deep voice, and he was never kind. As a kid, that was intimidating.

My aunt and uncle didn't have much money, but my father did. Whenever there were doctor bills or dental bills, he paid them. Once when I was in junior high school, I needed track shoes. Instead of him saying, "Okay, just drop Fred off, and we'll spend a day together and get the track shoes," he brings the money by, puts it in the mailbox, and leaves. The only time I would see him was at family functions, family reunions, things like this.

But I would always try to understand his situation. They would tell me stories about how much he had loved my mother. So I'm thinking, it must be hard for him to face me.

When I was a kid, I had a real bad nervous problem, and the psychologist told my aunt (who I called my mother) that he thought that I thought I was the cause of my mother's death. What a horrible thing to say, and what a horrible thing to let me know. I never thought that way. But I did think that was one reason my father couldn't be close. It bothered me more the older I got.

In junior high school, I ran track and played football. Those were good experiences. I was very successful in track, so I got to have the feeling of winning. Then I married my junior high school sweetheart. That's where a lot of things in my life started—some good things and some bad things. We were both in the twelfth grade when she got pregnant.

I didn't know what to do. I was scared. I remember sitting outside the doctor's office in the car by myself, waiting on the pregnancy test results.

Her mother hated me. She was the type of person who was into status, and I came around in a little raggedy '56 Plymouth that was rusted out. The other guy that Tina had dated was driving a brand-new car that year.

Her mother wanted this for her daughter—instead of me, who materially didn't have anything. But I felt like I had a lot more to offer inside.

Anyway, she didn't like me, so she's freaking out now thinking her daughter is pregnant. And her father's the same way. And I am just a nervous wreck. I mean, later on that night I got sick. I threw up and everything. Couldn't sleep for a couple of days. The whole thing was just real bad. And I'm thinking about college and all these things that you have to give up. And, of course, I know it's my fault, too.

In July of '66, my son was born. We moved out into our own apartment, and my wife got pregnant with my daughter.

Now, this is real important. My daughter was born in '68. In '69, we discovered a cyst on my wife's breast. She went to the hospital to have this cyst removed. I come to the hospital after work, and her mother is there. The mother who hates me. And my aunt is there. I come in, and everybody's crying. And Tina is there with all these tubes and things coming out of her, all this padding and stuff, and I don't know what's going on yet. Because I think maybe they put that there for removing her cyst, I don't know.

Then they tell me that she had a mastectomy. Well, oh my God. I lose it. I just lose it. And her mother snatched me by the arm and pulled me out in the hallway. She cursed me, saying this was all my fault. All my fault.

From that point on, my life changed like you would not believe. It was incredible. This was a beautiful, young black woman. I mean, just gorgeous. You know, nice breasts and a nice body.

Now you have a woman with one breast. I hate to say it that way, you know. But what do you do now? My aunt and uncle who raised me, they always seemed to care more about the other person than themselves. And a lot of that had rubbed off on me. I'm saying to myself, "You think you got it bad because you have to face your wife nude this way? How do you think your wife feels?" This is what I'm saying to myself.

I immediately stopped feeling sorry for myself and started feeling sorry for my wife. I thought, "This is my wife. This is the woman I love, and I'm going to make her feel as whole as possible." I did everything I could think of. I don't know where the strength came from. A lot of it came from God. I say that because I did a lot of praying and asking Him to help us both.

Well, we find that the cancer has spread. It was just a matter of time. We would have a little hope, and then it would come back, and then it would be a hysterectomy, and then it would be something else.

Tina handled it great. Not once did you ever see her sad. Not once did you ever see her crying about her condition. I can't explain it. She helped me. She helped everybody else around her get through this.

But to watch someone like that deteriorate before your eyes—it's incredible to have to go through something like that at a young age. Probably as a result, there are a whole lot of things that don't bother me today.

So she passed away. I don't care how much preparing you do...it was rough. It was real rough. And then trying to take care of two kids. I don't know how I did it. I like to think I was protected by God and by family.

When Tina and I first got married, I got a job through the Urban League working for a construction company in their art department printing blueprints. I took drafting and art courses in the evening. I had always been fascinated by—and always did well in—art classes at school. I was told I had a good eye.

After my wife died, the construction company sent me to college. I went for about a year, but I was just not in the right mind to do the work. I left there and went to work for a printing company as an assistant to the accountant. They had a real small art department, and the company was growing. I thought this would be great, to get into this art department on the ground floor.

I started dating. Now I know what women go through who are divorced single parents. You'll be out, and women approach you, and things are going along fine. The conversation is okay, and all of a sudden, "You have what? Two kids?"

At that time, I didn't want to make any commitments. First of all, I didn't want someone coming in who did not like my kids, or who my kids didn't like. I felt that they had been through enough. My whole life at that time was centered around my kids. It was all about them. They had to be okay. I didn't want anything else to hurt them. So I waited until my daughter was eighteen before I was willing to make a serious commitment.

And I didn't lose either one of them to whatever it is out there in the street. Because sometimes that happens to single parents. People always say, "Well, there's not a man there—that's why the kid got into trouble." The same thing can happen by not having a mother there.

I've been in photography for sixteen years now. I've always been fascinated by it. I took two photography courses just to learn the functions of the camera. I was in and out of the library and bookstores. And I was fortunate to have people come along in my life who were in photography and didn't mind sharing information with me.

A love started to develop here. I got to the point where all my extra money was going toward buying film and lenses. I was going to have to find a way to make money from this. I pawned some stuff and got the camera equipment I needed. I learned wedding photography working at the bridal department of a downtown department store. Later, I left the department store to work for a studio as a wedding and portrait photographer.

I met my second wife while I was still working at the printing company. She was white, so this was a totally new experience for me. When I first started working there, I wasn't interested in her, and she wasn't interested in me. We just went to lunch, you know? Just buddies.

After a while, we started to date. Then word got out, and there was some shock, and some surprise, but it was fine. There were no problems. Eventually, we moved in together. We lived together for nine years.

I asked her twice to marry me, and both times she turned me down. It was no big deal. We still lived together. We still loved one another. Then one day I got up to make coffee and give her breakfast in bed. It was a real lovey-dovey type day. I went back upstairs with the coffee and waited for the bacon to cook.

I was sitting on my side of the bed drinking my coffee. I leaned back on the pillow, and there was a ring box on the pillow. I said, "Wow. What is this?" And she's got this big grin on her face, you know? I open the box, and there is a ring. She was proposing to me. It was a great surprise.

This was one day in my life I'll never forget. I was so happy! Because this was what I really wanted to do. Naturally, I said yes. And, you know, I burned the bacon.

We never held hands in public. I just never did that. But that day, we did hold hands. We skipped. We hugged. It was one of the most beautiful days in my life. That was the beginning. I was in my late thirties by then.

A lot of my family hadn't met her, and a lot of her family hadn't met me. I wasn't nervous about getting married—I was nervous about these people getting along at the wedding. So I'm losing it. Her…it doesn't bother her. "It'll work out," she says. "Don't worry about it." The wedding was beautiful. Absolutely gorgeous. And everybody got along fine. Over in the corner, there was my oldest aunt with her oldest aunt. They're holding hands, and they're talking, you know. It was beautiful.

My divorce came as a surprise. I was forty-six when that happened. It devastated me, and I am still kind of dealing with it. Yes, we were having some problems, but I had been in it for the long haul.

One night we were out to dinner with some friends, and I thought we were having a great time. We had argued and stuff, but the dinner was nice. On the way home, she starts an argument, and it gets to the point where she is screaming at me. I can see the veins on her neck, and I'm thinking, "This is not right. Something is wrong here."

When we got home, I asked her, "Is this something we need to talk about?" She said, "Yes. You need a beer, and I'll bring your cigarettes." I got real nervous. Well, she dropped a bomb. "I want a divorce." I just lost it.

I had to photograph a wedding the next day. My wife, who I thought I would die with, had just told me she didn't want me anymore, and I had to go the very next day to photograph a wedding. And I'm crying. It was rough.

I almost broke down during the ceremony, but I don't think there was one person there who knew anything was wrong with me. I went in the back of the church, and I dug down deep and thought about the courage my first wife had. That's what got me through that wedding.

On the way home, I'm watching the sun set and crying my eyes out. I'm praying that she's going to be home, so I can maybe change her mind.

We talked, but it didn't change anything. This was May, and she didn't move out until August. Every day, every chance I could get, I'd ask, "Are you sure you don't want to change your mind?"

One day I'm mad and wondering why she's sticking around, wanting her to leave so I can start getting over it. Another day, I don't want her to leave.

Later, she told me she had been seeing someone for the past two years. It crushed me. I could not believe it. I asked her, "Did this friend know? Did that friend know?" She said everybody knew but me. The couple we went out with the night she told me she wanted a divorce knew. We had all laughed that night, drinking beer, having the best time. And all the time, they knew.

This is something that has affected me, ruined a good part of me, because now I'm unable to trust. And I hate that. I hate the side effects of that. I'm still the same loving, caring guy, but I'm more cautious now. I am a little colder toward relationships. It's not so easy to let people into my life.

The first Christmas I was by myself after the divorce, I bought myself a CD player on Christmas Eve. Now, you have to understand, this was real bad for me. This was my first Christmas without her, and our Christmases had been wonderful. Just us. If we saw any family, it was before or after.

Christmas Eve—I'm almost to the point of suicide here. The only thing I kept going back to was my first wife and her cancer. I kept thinking, "This divorce can't be as bad as that death." But it was. I hurt so bad.

I planned to do Christmas by myself. I planned a dinner all for me. Answer no phones. See no one. Nothing. I put the answering machine on two rings. You can imagine—my family loves me, and I got all kinds of Merry Christmas messages. I cried when my daughter was leaving her message on the answering machine.

I had bought six CDs. One of them was Patti LaBelle, and one was Gladys Knight. You know the songs they sing, those slow love songs. Deep. Heart things. I played that music. I wanted it as rough as I could get it. Patti LaBelle sings one song about losing people and getting sad, but don't get sad because they wouldn't want you to do that. I thought about my first wife, who had died, and my mother, who had died, and about my second wife.

I cried for hours. I looked at my gun. I thought about it. I feel like I accomplished something by not picking it up. But it was dangerous. It was real dangerous, and I would never recommend it to anyone. The way I set it up, I told lies to my family, told them that I would come by. If they had known what I was doing, they would have been knocking on the door. They would have sent the police over. I will tell them one day. I want to understand it better first. I'm not a psychologist. I didn't know why I needed to do this.

Afterwards, though, it was like this huge burden had been lifted off me. The next Christmas I was fine. I was sad, but I was fine. I didn't build my life around getting her back, and I didn't feel like I had to have somebody right away to replace her. That can make your life miserable. Now I'm enjoying my freedom and living by myself. It's been three years since the divorce.

Being by myself is one of the greatest things that has happened to me. It's allowed me to know Fred. It's allowed me to deal with my divorce. There's peace of mind there. This may sound kind of selfish, but I like having that space and not having to share it. I feel like all my life I've been around people. I've never been alone. This is new.

I like being able to put the toilet paper on inside or outside. I like leaving the toilet seat up. I want my home to be peaceful, and I work real hard at it. I figure that's probably the only thing I have control over. I've always let my wife, or other women in my life, control the home.

The very first thing I did when my wife left was change the entire house. I repainted everything. I rearranged the furniture. I changed the colors of every room. Put wallpaper up. I didn't know how to do any of this stuff. I went to the library, got books, asked people.

We had never had blinds, so I put blinds on every window. Getting rid of her mark and reestablishing mine. I got real emotional putting the wallpaper up and painting. Because I knew this was part of getting rid of her.

Last year, I cut the birch tree down that we planted together, and wow, what a relief. That tree was just about dead when I cut it down. I kept associating that tree with our relationship. Cutting that tree down was like cutting the umbilical cord after all those years. Because I'd always look out my window and see that tree, and I'd always think of her.

I've started to enjoy more things by myself, and I've started to find out more about myself. I took a trip last year to stay in a cabin in the Grand Tetons. The day I woke up to leave on the trip, any tension I had from my life was just gone. I felt free. Just getting in the car and cranking the key, I felt nothing could bother me.

That was probably the freest I've ever felt in my life. I just realized how good I felt, how happy I was. I rode down the highway with the windows down, and I put my jazz on, and I sang.

I think having these years being by myself has helped me to be a little stronger emotionally. Because I was a mess there for a while. Some people seek out psychologists, and there were people who were telling me I should do that, but I chose to be by myself. I think the route I took was good for me.

I have always had confidence in my work. The camera has always given me that confidence. But outside of work is where I lacked it. During my second marriage, I was always told I wasn't smart enough, that I couldn't do anything right. And I think after years and years, that stuff beats you down. It gets in your head, and you start thinking it's true.

Like at work, it used to be if something happened I didn't like or agree with, I wouldn't say anything. I was afraid if I said something someone would think I was militant or arrogant. I'd keep it bottled up inside me, and I'd go home and have headaches and stomachaches. The doctor even put me on Xanax for a while. And I finally said, "Wait a minute. I'm going to let this stuff out."

For example, I've had a problem at work with my ideas being accepted. I've set out ideas that were ignored, then seen those same ideas come from someone else and be accepted. Now when that happens I say, "I tried to get you to do that months ago. Why didn't you listen to me?" It feels real good. I got all this confidence from just being by myself. I just made the decision that I'm getting in the driver's seat, I'm driving the car. It's my life. I'm taking control. Now I feel stronger, a lot stronger. Now I can walk anywhere without that camera and feel the same way as I do with it.

I'm engaged now. This is the hardest thing, because I'm trying to trust again. I've always been able to love. I've always been able to give. But trusting is real hard. I tell her all the time, "Please understand what I've been through. If you trust me and you love me, eventually it's going to work out. But you have to take me by the hand. I'm just like a little baby."

If there's a problem in my life right now, it's that. So I just work with my head, and with my feelings, and I try to fall back on how I believe she feels for me, and it goes away. But then it comes back. People say you should try to hold your feelings back, but I don't believe you can.

This is scary for me. But we've known each other for fourteen years, so I'm going for it. This is the decision I've made, and I feel like it's a good decision—and if it doesn't work, it doesn't mean it was a bad decision. Because everything's a lesson. I think people who don't give love and receive love, they're missing out on something. If nothing else, I feel good about knowing that.

I love getting older. I think it's because of the knowledge you gain. I like to think I make better decisions. I have more grey in my hair. I have a few wrinkles. I like to think I'm beyond my looks, which is what I depended on when I was younger. And I look forward to being a grandfather even though neither of my kids is married yet. I don't have a problem about getting old.

I'm already planning to spend my fiftieth birthday by myself. It may sound selfish, but I don't think we do enough for ourselves, and I just want to get ready for the next era. We're not here for very long, you know.

Papa Joe

Joe Kunz

> I like living here. I know that part of it is living with Gail. I would put my life in her hands without batting an eye. I've never been this way. I was born in July. I'm a Cancer, a crab. I have my shell. I don't approach something forward—I sidle around it. I've always had shells within shells within shells protecting me. With Gail, I've never felt any need for shells.

The saltbox farmhouse that Joe Kunz, a sixty-one-year-old CIA retiree, shares with his wife, Gail, is encircled by several gardens, outbuildings, and a house trailer where his stepdaughter lives with her family. Stalks of corn and sunflowers stand like sentinels in the cold, snow-covered field.

Inside the house, the warm blue-and-white country kitchen restores us from the cold January day outside. A noteboard on the wall says, "Papa will pick up kids at one p.m." Crystals hang in a nearby window, reflecting the occasional winter sunlight.

As we look at a wall covered by family pictures, Joe offers us raisin-cinnamon bread he has made from a recipe given to him by an Amish farmer. Gail tells us how he took her grown daughter to the hospital when she had her first child and stayed with her through the delivery. Gail says about his relationship to his stepchildren, "He's just here for them."

Joe is a tall, robust man with an erect carriage. He has curly white hair, clear blue eyes, and a ruddy complexion. He wears a blue cableknit sweater, jeans, and house slippers, and drinks Postum from a large mug with "Papa" on the side. Joe speaks in a deep, resonant voice about a crisis period in his late thirties and about the relationships that have influenced him.

Two people have been crucial to Joe's life: his intense, domineering father and his loving, nurturing wife. An idyllic early childhood was cut short by his father, who used Joe and his brothers to help fulfill his ambition to become a successful farmer. Although Joe, like his brothers, left home in anger when he came of age, he carried with him a penchant for work that contributed to a major breakdown in midlife.

Joe's childhood was overshadowed by his father's negativity, but his later years have been blessed with joy. In retirement, he became reconciled with his parents through taking care of them in the years before they died. And he has found a healing love with his wife of the past ten years. Gail has brought warmth and stability to their relationship, and has opened him up to feelings of deep trust for the first time in his life.

In late midlife, Joe has found contentment in marriage and family life. And his passion for gardening provides a connection to nature, which brought him such happiness when he was a small boy.

My family lived in Arizona during the Depression. I was just a baby at the time. We had a very good life. My father was a fruit-and-vegetable huckster. He always said he never made less than $50 a week right through the worst of the Depression. We ate very well—the finest fruits and vegetables. Everything was just wonderful, but my dad wanted to go back to Indiana. He was probably going through some kind of midlife crisis. He was forty years old, and he wanted in the worst way to come back to Indiana.

Instead of coming straight to Indiana, my parents thought it would be a good time to show the children the West. So we spent approximately three months traveling around. And this was not all sightseeing because, in order to make our way, my dad—and sometimes the older two or three boys— would work as itinerant farm laborers. I was three or four by that time.

I remember so many things. The smell of the alfalfa fields and the asphalt highways, and of the big trucks that would go by. For fifteen or twenty years after that, the smell of a highway in the summertime would take me right back to California. The smell of an alfalfa field would do that, too. I could almost see those fields, and see the mountains, and see California.

I remember standing by the Pacific Ocean and my brother, who was about ten, saying that those waves came all the way from China, those waves that seemed as high as a house. I remember being above the clouds, in the mountains. It was a really, really happy time.

When we came back to Indiana, the bad times started. We lived for two years in a log house without electricity, basically without any money or any kind of income. So it was a very difficult time. Once a year, we got two pairs of pants and two shirts and a pair of shoes. That's what you wore for the school year. And that would come out of the chicken money my mother earned.

Every cent my father could beg or borrow, he put back into the farm. My mother tried and tried and tried to get him to give it up and go back to the Southwest, where they had lived a good life. But he saw these seven sons as his labor force on his way to becoming a big Indiana farmer, which is what he always wanted.

I remember my parents arguing, arguing, arguing over this. I was terrified by it. I was terrified by a lot of things. I was terrified by the thought of the end of the world because my father believed that the world might come to an end at just any time. As a child, I can remember him talking about this with the next-door neighbor, until all hours of the night.

And I can remember, when I was a few years older, lying out in the grass. We would sleep outside when it was too hot to sleep in the house. I would look up at the stars and wonder when the stars were going to come crashing down to earth and burn us all up. You didn't know when God was going to kill everybody or when the end of the world was going to come. It was just terrifying to think like this.

And we would have family worship, which would last for an hour a day. My father would read the Bible, and we would all pray. Every day. On Sunday, we would go to church two or three times. And there would be prayer meetings at least once during the week.

When I got to be about thirteen or so, my father bought a new piece of farm machinery. He gave me the instruction manual and told me it was my job to take care of it. I was really proud. By the time I was sixteen or seventeen, I was in charge of all the machinery, a hired hand, and baling hay over a large area. I was a man.

Looking back, there are so many things that I learned from being around my father all day long. These are the things I really know. I learned how to work and how to take responsibility from a very early age. Later in my life I ended up cracking up, I was such a good worker.

I knew that when I was eighteen I would leave home. I had watched my older brothers, who had all rebelled, who had all nearly killed my father in one way or another, and then they would leave home.

It's just that our father was such a domineering person. It's impossible to explain how hard he was on us, how hard he made us work. There was never any time for anything other than the farm, anything other than work.

After college, I went to D.C. and became a federal employee with the CIA. I worked very, very hard. I worked twenty-four-hour days, never took any time off. Then, when I was thirty-eight years old, I went to this week-long employee training seminar, which turned into an encounter session.

In the course of the week, I became more and more disillusioned with our organization. I found out that the people from communications felt that communications would be the downfall of the organization. People from operations, they felt that operations was bad, and people from other divisions felt the same way about their part. I thought I was working for a real elite government organization. I thought we were really accomplishing something. I suddenly realized that everybody else there thought their department was bad. It was a shattering experience.

At the end of the week at the training seminar, I had been selected to give our team's report. So around midnight, when everybody else was asleep, I did the sort of thing I used to do back in college. I stayed up the rest of the night writing my report, which I had to give about nine o'clock Saturday morning.

I worked and I worked and I worked, and I wrote page after page after page of my report. I got very sleepy. It was about five o'clock in the morning. I decided I was finished. I snapped out the light, and I crawled into my bed.

All of a sudden, there was this light. It was pitch black, but there was this light. And it was kind of milky and kind of blood-streaked, and it started to get bigger. I saw it with my eyes closed. It scared the hell out of me. I jumped out of bed.

I thought I was losing my mind. I turned the light on. I was going to stay up the rest of the night. But I got very, very sleepy, and finally I couldn't stay up anymore. I crawled back into bed and turned the light off. Maybe ten minutes later, the same thing happened again. The light got bigger and bigger and bigger until it was all around me. And I felt this tugging sensation like I was being tugged out of a sleeping bag. It was very frightening. Then I fell asleep. And I had no idea what this meant.

There were other incidents over the next three or four days, and things got more and more chaotic. I can't be sure, but I think that on the seventh day, or something like that, I got picked up on the street because I was without any shoes, and I don't know that I had any clothes on except a raincoat. I certainly didn't have any identification on me. Anyway, I didn't know my name. They didn't know who I was. And I wasn't speaking.

They took me to a neighborhood clinic of some sort. A woman counselor talked to me, and finally I was able to say a word. And another word. It was like I was so completely withdrawn that I was mute. I was like a child, I was so completely shrunk in. But within a matter of fifteen to twenty minutes, I was able to speak in complete sentences.

I knew who I was, and I realized what was going on. I told them who they had to call, because my organization has a special psych staff of doctors. They called them, and I was taken to the hospital where they put our people who crack up.

After another couple of months or so, they decided I was okay, and they let me go back to work. Within a few more months, I was right back into the swing of things, which meant that I was working long hours, traveling, and had no social life.

A year later, I decided to go back to Indiana, and I was crazy as a loon. I thought the devil was after me. Things were backwards. I was going through red lights and stopping at green lights, for example. I followed this woman driving a gold Cadillac right into an Oldsmobile dealership. I was crazy. I can't remember what all I did, only that I had so much energy.

I didn't want to go back to another hospital, but they finally convinced me to go, and I was there two-and-a-half weeks. I went on a couple of day passes, then got out of there and drove back to D.C.

By this time, I knew my career was finished. It was 1973. They put me on sick leave and offered me disability retirement, and I retired. That was twenty-one years ago. That is my change-of-life story.

Now why did this happen? My personal conclusion is that my life had reached a kind of crisis point. Looking back on it, I think there were all kinds of things that entered into what happened to me. I had been disappointed in a relationship with a girl that I wanted to marry when I was around thirty-three. I had decided that I wasn't going to go through the pain of that again, so I hadn't dated for six years. I was working very hard, sometimes day and night, becoming disillusioned with what was going on at work. Because if you invest your life in something...

For example, I remember all the things we did as little kids to fight the war. We collected scrap iron and milkweed pods, saved our dimes for war stamps and war bonds. And we had a scrap pile twenty feet high in the middle of the school yard. After that was growing up, and thinking we were going to fight the communists, and eventually going into government service. I viewed it as, "I'm one of the good guys, and we're trying to save our country and the world from evil communism."

And then to come to this point in my life at thirty-eight or thirty-nine years old, to find out that I was part of a pretty screwed-up organization.

After that, I went out West to live. I lived in Colorado. I lived in Washington state and California. All my life, I'd had a kind of a dream. I'd wanted to get back the feeling I had when I was a child in California.

But I could not recapture the overwhelming sights and feelings of my childhood. I drove the coastal highway from San Diego to Canada, but never again saw the waves twenty feet high that my brothers said came all the way from China. I drove the back roads to hunt for the camps of migrant farm workers. I crossed the Golden Gate and Bay bridges, I revisited the big trees in Yosemite and Sequoia parks. But nothing quite fit.

Around 1980, my father called me home. He was quitting farming and had sold his machinery. My dad was around eighty and was getting kind of senile. He got lost in his car way out at one side of the county at three or four o'clock in the morning, and the sheriff brought him home. So my sister and I decided to move my parents' house trailer up there to her place, with the agreement that I would live with my sister and brother-in-law and look after my folks.

I nursed my parents roughly the last ten years of their lives, becoming more and more responsible for them. I fed them. I wiped their butts. I shaved my father, helping him in different ways like that until he died. I had to put him into a nursing home eventually, go to see him two or three times a week, watch him die of cancer.

And then, after he died, I had three-and-a-half years with my mother down here. I had a baby intercom in my bedroom and over in her trailer. And so, at two or three o'clock in the morning, I'd hear, "Joe, Joe, Joe!" And I'd jump up, put some clothes on, and stagger over to see what was wrong with her. I'd feed her, give her massages every night.

Okay, that all sounds like it was a burden on me. The thing I want to say is that those ten years brought me full circle back to my parents. When I left home at age eighteen, I swore I would never go back again. I was so angry about growing up the way I did, being limited the way I was, being forced to go to church—everything. I was so angry that, for the next three years, I would not even go home for Christmas.

To show you how angry I was, I told people I would never marry until my mother died because I did not want my wife ever to meet my mother. I said that. I said that if my mother were walking down the street and I was across the street walking the other way, I wouldn't even stop. This was in my twenties. But when you get older, you learn a little bit more.

I can remember the first time I won an argument with my father. I was probably thirty-five, and I was strong and mentally sharp. My father was past seventy. He was failing. I was taking my mother's side in this argument about family finances, and I used every trick I had ever heard my father use in an argument.

I won the argument, and my dad cried. I had never seen my dad cry in my life. Tears came out my dad's eyes. And I felt like a shit. And I realized that for thirty-five years I'd been struggling against my father, and finally I'd beaten him. And I felt like a shit. In front of his wife, I beat him. I might as well have taken a whip to him. I had been a good son. I had learned all my dad's techniques in arguing, and now I had won. I, in my pride and strength, had beaten up a feeble old man.

Anyhow, this was an extremely valuable ten-year period. I learned so much about myself. I learned how I was like my parents. When I saw the source of my good traits, I came to accept my parents with increasing pride, for I am very proud of my accomplishments. When I saw the source of the things I don't like about myself, I forgave them and myself.

When I had accepted my faults, it was easier to allow others to discover them. Hiding my mother from any potential wife was no longer so important. I no longer tried so hard to present myself as a world-traveling sophisticate with a genius IQ who had been everywhere, done everything, knew everything—but was scared someone would see inside me, inside my shells.

I learned so much about my parents in the ten years of caring for them when they were old. As I did more for them, I came to accept them better and even to love them, in the sense that love is an emotion in which the happiness of the loved one is essential to one's own happiness. I have long realized that helping someone you don't like makes you like them. The key to accepting my parents was caring for them in their old age.

Twelve years ago I was presented with the answer to a lifetime of longing and searching. I was rewarded for caring for my parents one day by this gal driving in there to visit my sister. Two months later, we were married. We came down here and bought this place and have lived happily ever after. To me, it's kind of an interesting story.

She was somebody I had known about for thirty years. She had gone through nurses' training with my sister. We had some of the same friends and went to the same churches, but we had never seen each other. She got married, had four children, divorced, and here we were in our late forties or early fifties when she came up to visit my sister.

One morning I went out to milk my cow at six or seven o'clock, and she was out taking an early morning walk. She came up and said, "Hi, I'm Gail Croft." It didn't take more than a day or so. I had never had a relationship easy like this, so easy.

I spent the following weekend with her. Came away very satisfied that I was going to change my life. The weekend was fantastic. Didn't know that there was that much left in a fifty-year-old man. We never made it to a restaurant, we never made it to the movies, we never made it out of bed for twenty-four hours. I couldn't believe it.

About three months after we were married, she was having the after-the-holiday blahs. I said, "Call in sick, and we'll just go for a drive in the country."

We had been thinking about buying land and then building on it, so we drove down here to see a farm we heard was for sale. We came down here and walked over the land, and went back and put a deposit down on it and bought it. We have lived happily ever after. Ten years we've lived in this place, and for me, the last ten years have been the happiest of my life.

Been living here, gardening. That's about it. I've had big gardens, huge gardens, no sense, no rhyme or reason to it—I just like to grow things. One time I bought twenty kinds of radishes, and I put twenty rows of radishes in. I wanted to find out which radishes I liked best.

Now I read a lot, too. I can't tell you what all I've done. I built a barn back here. Still working on it. Got a dog here three years ago, bred her, and kept a couple of her puppies, so I walk the dogs twice a day. I started tutoring high school kids in math. I enjoy that. And there've always been grandkids around. I don't get bored very easily. I'm egotistical enough that I don't get bored with my own company.

That's my life. I enjoy the feel of this place. I like living here. I know that part of it is living with Gail. It feels good having her around. I would put my life in her hands without batting an eye.

I've never been this way. I was born in July. I'm a Cancer, a crab. I have my shell. I don't approach something forward—I sidle around it. I've always had shells within shells within shells protecting me. With Gail, I've never felt any need for shells.

I've learned a lot since we got married. One of the things is that disposable diapers don't burn. I was a true fifty-year-old bachelor. I'm different from a lot of men. I have never desired children of my own, even though I wanted to have a wife and a family and a nice house.

I have sixteen nieces and nephews. Thirty years of having nieces and nephews made it easy for me to become a "papa." It was not difficult for me to feel like these children are my grandchildren. In a very real sense, they are my grandchildren. They came into the world since I've been in Gail's life.

Our farm is the gathering place for our nineteen-member extended family. The kids all like to come here—and the grandkids. They cry when they have to leave. There is something so much fun about being down here. I can't put my finger on what it is. We have to beat some of these kids off with a stick.

It makes me feel proud, and it's so good to know that they like it that much. I think living here approaches a state of grace.

Living with Questions

Marty Lynch

I'm trapped, and if I want to get out of this trap, I'm going to have to make sacrifices that maybe I'm not wanting to make, like giving up my house and scaling back my lifestyle a bit. So maybe I'm not really as bad off as some days I think I am. I kind of go up and down. One of these days, I'll figure out what I want to do. And I'll go do it. I keep asking the questions. It's important to keep doing that.

Marty Lynch comes to talk with us at a mutual friend's newly acquired home, located in a quiet Southern suburb. It's a Sunday afternoon in early May, but the sights and smells of summer are already apparent. As we walk over the property, we talk casually about the landscaping projects that our friend is working on. It's obvious that Marty is very knowledgeable about plants and trees and bushes.

Marty is about five-foot-six with a slender frame. His sandy-colored hair, stylishly cut, falls over his tanned forehead. Deep lines cut the corners of his large, light blue eyes, and his close beard is beginning to gray. He wears a white T-shirt with a marathon ad on it, purple running shorts, and white Nikes.

Gardening and landscaping, as well as a happy marriage, are the mainstays of Marty's life right now. Although born into a financially comfortable family, he has survived his share of traumas, including an abusive father, the Kent State riot, and the loss of his first wife to brain cancer. His long-term career in public health has turned into "a frustrating, dead-end job."

Now, at forty-five, Marty is trying to determine what he wants to do with his future and how to balance his need for job satisfaction with his need for job security. It's a painful period of questioning, when answers either seem to contradict each other or are not forthcoming, especially when he feels that he doesn't have the self-confidence he needs to find the answers. Marty's grace is that he knows he must continue, for now, to live with the questions.

I was born in Cleveland, Ohio, in 1949. Pretty much grew up in an upper-middle-class neighborhood in suburbia. I have a sister two years older and a sister five years younger.

My parents hated each other, but they were good Catholics, so they didn't separate, "for the good of the children." Didn't ever see any real love in the house. I spent a lot of energy in my childhood trying to get my father's approval and never getting it.

My father was real verbally abusive. He went to a Jesuit university, and he was always spouting either this military or this Jesuit nonsense. "I'm the lord of my castle." "This and that are off limits" and "You are shiftless individuals." Very, very strange. I don't even begin to understand it. As a result, I never got to know him, and he never got to know me.

Dinner was the time we got picked on. It's funny because I eat extremely fast today, still. Both my sisters do as well. We talk about that, usually when we're sitting down at a meal, and we're eating so fast. We realize why we do it, yet we can't stop doing it.

My mother was probably—I know this from conversations we had over the years—she was real protective because she didn't perceive my father as having much of a relationship with me. I think my mother tried to compensate for that.

A lot that still centers me—like my appreciation for birds and flowers—my mom instilled in me. I remember one time going on a bird walk through the metropolitan park system with her. I remember traipsing through the mud and looking at this weird little guy, a ruby-crowned king. Years later, here I am doing all these same things. I have a life list of birds.

Other memories. I remember sitting in ninth-grade English class when John Kennedy was killed. And I remember my respect for Bobby Kennedy, who probably made me think of myself as political for the first time. I was a senior in high school, and I was starting to realize what Vietnam was really about.

Bobby Kennedy was probably the first politician to say, "Not all wars are glorious, and this one isn't, and we've made a mistake here." And probably because my own butt was on the line, I heard those things. Bobby Kennedy getting killed was the first time somebody really took a chip off my political optimism. Like a lot of us at that time. We had these ideals.

I remember the cities burning the summer before I went off to college. Cleveland had riots. Just as a curiosity, we drove down to see all the National Guard troops in the black neighborhood, which we called "the area" in those days. Seeing all those things had a lot to do with who I became, because I was from this pretty conservative, upper-middle-class background. My parents, I'm sure, were always Republican. My sisters and I have always been flaming liberals.

Two years later, I was at Kent State University when the riot occurred. People have this image of Kent as this hotbed of radical activity, like Berkeley. But it wasn't. It was a conservative land-grant college in Ohio, for goodness sake! The riot was terrible, and I got caught up in the middle of it.

I was literally standing right next to somebody who had his head blown off. My roommate and I, we went up and tried to help this person—he had this fifteen-foot trail of blood coming out of his head. My roommate took off his jacket and covered the head, and we were going to pick this person up and put him on the grass. Why? I don't know why, but that's what we were fixing to do.

When we tried to do that, my hand went up under the head, and there was no other half of the head. Then a pepper-gas canister went off at my feet, and I just kind of crawled across this parking lot, and by the time my eyes cleared, I saw a woman whose chest was ripped open from a bullet that just fragmented through her body.

At that point, I was able to get up and run, and I ran across this parking lot to my dormitory. I remember going up to my room, and there was a bottle of Chloraseptic there, and I threw it through this mirror out of frustration. I guess I cried for about an hour.

That whole summer I spent in Washington, D.C., raising money for the kids who had gotten shot, because the insurance companies were not settling. Kent had been declared a riot. Insurance companies don't have to pay in a riot. It was an interesting learning experience for me.

At school, I could still—there were some weeds that grew all summer long and gave off the smell of tear gas—I could still smell tear gas. The sound of helicopters still danced in my brain and made me think about all that stuff. I hadn't put enough in perspective yet, and I wasn't ready to crack the books.

So that fall I took an upper-division sociology course called the Akron Neighborhood Faculty Program. It was a very interesting course. It was thirty hours a week of pure experience, no books. What we were doing was going into the inner city, living in and among the people who had to live off the public trough, so to speak. We'd spend time with welfare mothers. We'd spend time in the rat-control program office to learn what they did.

We'd spend time in the welfare office to see all the hoops they made the people jump through.

I remember talking with a woman who was eighty-five years old. All she could do any more was read—that was her only pleasure in life—and her glasses were broken. And in those days, in the welfare system, glasses weren't paid for.

Most guys my age remember the first draft lottery and how tough that was—1970, I think it was. I don't know if you've talked to any other guys who had the same type of experience. We all kind of made light of it, but the draft was scary. Particularly if you had already come to the point of view that the war was wrong. I thought, "Are you going to have the courage of your convictions and say, 'No, I won't go' and go to jail? Or are you just going to run?"

Those are the decisions we were all faced with. There's no way I would have gone, not in a million years. I know that today. And that was hard. You have to remember, we had all those things pulling at us because, for people from our parents' generation, war was glorious. They had saved the world from tyranny.

I already told you that I spent my childhood trying to get my father's approval and never getting it. As a result of that, I've not had any relationship with my father as an adult. I didn't even talk to him for about fifteen years. Not because I was angry. Just because I had stopped trying, and he never did try.

In all honesty, there probably was a lot of anger there in the early part of my life, but as time went on, it didn't make any sense to be angry anymore. It had no relevance to my life.

My father's still alive. But even if we were to agree tomorrow that we were going to carve out some sort of relationship, it would be like a relationship with a stranger. To be honest about it, there's not a lot there that we could pick up from. I can't tell you how many ways that affects my life today.

Not because I'm looking for his approval anymore. But I still remember all those times in my life when it would have been nice to have had the guidance of an older male figure who could have helped me through some difficulty, saying, "I've been though this, and this is what I did, and this was the result." I've never had that reassurance.

And I've missed that. I constantly battle that. I have to screw up my courage all the time. I'm real tentative anytime I get into a new situation.

It's lack of self-confidence, that's all it is. And I know it, and I know where it comes from. And I know it shouldn't make any difference anymore. But it does. I don't know how you beat that. I don't think you ever do.

Since my first wife died, it's been more and more of a problem. I guess, when you lose your partner for life, you lose your self-concept, too, and that takes its toll.

My first wife was my childhood sweetheart. She was fourteen and I was seventeen, and we fell madly in love. Stayed madly in love. Went together all through high school. Broke up for a couple of years in college, but got back together again as soon as I got done with college. We were married for thirteen years, and we were still madly in love when she got sick.

We were about as close as you can be. Went through all of life's most embarrassing moments together, like first sexual experiences. Laura really was—she really, truly was—my best friend. She literally did grow up with me. It was a great relationship, a relationship of equals.

Laura died a horrible, horrible death. She had a brain tumor. She woke up one morning with a little numbness in her hand, a little numbness in her foot. She said she had noticed that she was stumbling over some words. I said, "That sounds neurological. You'd better get that evaluated right away."

The neurologist told her she had MS-type symptoms, but milder, some virus like MS that would run its course. She shouldn't worry about it. We went off on vacation, and I started to notice Laura couldn't tell right from left anymore. We immediately looked further into what the hell was going on.

Laura got an MRI, and it was a tumor in the center of her brain. It was obvious that she wasn't going to live. She spent five-and-a-half weeks in the hospital, doing all the appropriate studies, blah, blah, blah. They put her through radiation. And then sent her home, basically to die. Little by little by little each day.

Cancer does not leave you any dignity. As a spouse, you're bound and determined you're going to save some dignity for this person that you love. People have said to me that they thought I did that for her. I said, "I don't think so. You weren't there for all the ugliness."

You do the best you can. I can't begin to imagine the terror that Laura had to be going through. I couldn't talk to her about it. It was always a one-sided conversation because she couldn't talk. I had to be the one who told her she was going to die.

Yeah, Laura and I were high school sweethearts, and she knew why I ticked the way I ticked without my explaining it to her. It takes a lot of years to achieve that in a relationship, and we achieved it at a fairly early age.

It's like losing an arm to lose that person. It's like losing a part of yourself. It's physical pain. I can't explain it to you. It's not just emotional, or it's so deeply emotional that it *feels* physical. I think I cried every day for a year after she died.

I also did a little running away. It was a good way to go through the grieving process. I took a trip to the South Pacific. I went to Australia, New Zealand, strung together a bunch of adventure vacations, had some fun for about four months. When I got back home, I didn't work for about another year.

I thought about what I wanted to do. Did I want to start my own business? Did I want to go back and do the same thing I had been doing? I thought a lot, but I also got in shape and had fun. I was swimming a mile-and-a-half every day and bicycling thirty miles and then running five miles, doing mini-triathlons, just keeping body and soul together, running away. I was trying to figure out how I was going to restart things, how I was going to rebuild my life.

I ended up taking a job back doing what I had always been doing, just because it was comfortable. The job, at least, was secure.

Since college, I've been in the public-health field. First started out as a VD investigator and did a lot of street work talking with pimps and prostitutes about their lives. Going to find their shady sex partners in these various holes in the wall and crack houses and shooting galleries. It was interesting because you have to wear a lot of different hats and play a lot of different roles to get people to tell you what you need to know.

It was just the line of work I ended up in. I've worked for various state agencies or the federal government in different cities. Got promotions along the way. I started at the very grassroots of public health, and now I'm at the national level, doing assessments of public health programs.

I think I've reached my level of incompetence, the Peter Principle. I really belong out there talking to people in the streets, but now, instead, I'm a damn bureaucrat going to inane meetings. Talking about nonsense all day. It's so unfulfilling, so unsatisfying.

My garden looks great, though. That's what I put my heart into. Laura's dying did tend to make me take life a little less seriously. It made me a little less type-A. Things that would really bother me in the past—say a work situation—now it's, like, who gives a damn in the grand scheme of things?

On the other hand, I'm really bumping up heavy against middle age now. In all honesty, I think I started bumping up against that much earlier than a lot of my friends because I didn't have kids to divert my attention from me.

Of course, when Laura got sick, my life went on hold until she died. And then it took a couple of years to rebuild it. And in rebuilding it, I went back to something that was comfortable, which was this job I had been doing for years and years and years. And I had forgotten that I left it because I hated it. I should have remembered that.

Yeah, so I'm bumping up real hard against being forty-five. What I really want to do is be a gardener. I just prefer being outside. I get the love of plants from my mom, although I picked up gardening on my own. But gardening or landscaping would pay me only about $10,000 a year and all the dirt I can eat. Therefore, I'm a bureaucrat.

I've been married to Sally for more than five years now. I met her in Florida in 1987 at a track-club banquet. I got thrust into singleness when Laura died. Dating? I didn't even remember how to do that stuff. I felt so ridiculous.

But Sally and I had all these things in common. We did scuba diving, we ran, we did triathlons, we were doing all the same things. So we had lots of things to talk about, and it's worked out real well.

But it still doesn't replace what I lost. I really feel like Laura's death was the death of my youth. I was only thirty-seven years old when she died, but that had been the person I was with for my whole youth. That's how I regarded it.

Laura's death is the most important thing that's ever happened to me and the most devastating. Some days I still don't feel like I've recovered from that. It's been seven years. Some days I feel fine, and other days...I don't know. It shook my foundations. To get centered back from that is a real battle.

I guess the other thing that has framed the last fifteen years for me is running. I became a physical being at about thirty years old. I quit smoking and picked up running. Prior to that, I wasn't into sports. I wasn't a jock in school, didn't play organized sports.

But at thirty years old, I decided to start jogging to lose a little weight, and that led to quitting smoking. Then, about a year-and-a-half ago, I developed a foot problem that has prevented me from running consistently.

Running every day has a mental health component to it, and all of a sudden, that's gone.

And I'm in this dead-end job that's giving me no satisfaction. And I'm bumping against being middle-aged and all that comes with that. It's not been a real good year, or year-and-a-half. I don't know what I'm going to do with all this. You've caught me at a bad time.

I'm not going to go out and buy a pastel-colored sports car and run away. That's not what I'm going to do. I'm asking questions, but I don't have a clue. It's easier to...what's the Pink Floyd song? Something about becoming "comfortably numb." It's easier to become comfortably numb than it is to face all this and start over.

I don't know what the answer is. Some days, I feel like I could stand up and pee on the desk and walk out. Sing three bars of "Alice's Restaurant" and keep on going. And then—other days, obviously—my need-for-security side says, "Well gee, Marty, you know, they are paying you a better salary than you can go out and generate on your own in the immediate future. And you have this house note." You know, those typical forty-five-year-old things.

My brain keeps pulling me toward doing some sort of little business, like a lawn-maintenance business, but I don't know if I will or not. I'm a government worker. Let's just say that there's not a real big pool of risk-takers among government workers. I know that about myself. I was out of work, had plenty of money, plenty of time to start a business, and I didn't. I had internal business to take care of, and I just wasn't ready then.

I'm trapped and, if I want to get out of this trap, I'm going to have to make sacrifices that maybe I'm not wanting to make, like giving up my house and scaling back my lifestyle a bit. So maybe I'm not really as bad off as some days I think I am. I kind of go up and down.

One of these days, I'll figure out what I want to do. And I'll go do it. Meanwhile, I keep asking the questions. It's important to keep doing that.

A Bad Picker Makes Good

Stefan Marks

> After figuring out the codependency stuff, I seemed to get my life under control. I started listening to what people were saying to me. We may know six hundred people, for example, 595 who like us and five who don't. And we tend to spend ninety-five percent of our energy on those five jerks and forget about the other 595. That's not smart. I let go of all the negativity and of the negative people in my life. What a genius! I was only forty-five when I figured this one out. Not bad, huh?

Stefan Marks breaks all of the stereotypes we usually associate with accountants. He's Clark Gable handsome, Groucho Marx funny, Robin Williams exuberant. His house, built on the shore of a Midwestern lake, looks like a setting for a romantic Hollywood movie circa 1950.

As he gives us a tour, Stefan points out a couple of his paintings. It's clear that he has a creative gift for capturing the natural environment. He also shows us his newborn West Highland puppies, born just one week ago. He tells us he's been studying books on how to raise them.

Stefan's family background explains, in part, his unconventionality. His father, a math whiz and a physical giant, put his talents to work for the gambling syndicate in Chicago. Stefan grew up under his father's powerful shadow. His awareness both of being different and of wanting to be like others trapped him in a conflict that had emotional and physical consequences.

Ever since he was a teenager, Stefan has fought Crohn's Disease, which weakens the autoimmune system and which eventually led to a serious codeine dependency that he battled and overcame in his early fifties. A few years before this, he had begun to understand and deal with his codependent behavior, which had influenced the break up of his three marriages.

At fifty-five, Stefan has become more self-reflective and self-aware. He is learning to live with his disease. A regular workout schedule helps him keep in good physical shape and handle stress. He still enjoys dating, but has also found a special pleasure in living alone and doing things he enjoys by him-self, such as fishing and painting. He has discovered that being a good person begins with taking care of oneself.

Stefan says he's a happy guy—and he's very convincing.

I was born on February 21, 1939, on Chicago's west side, a pretty tough area. We lived in an apartment over a delicatessen. I remember the floor was slanted. My dad went out and bought me a train, and I ran the train under the card table where all the ladies played mah-jongg. I was always a sickly kid growing up. I had asthmatic hay fever.

My mother was this nice Jewish woman with blond hair, doing every-thing right. She was a little bit like Gracie Allen. On my mother's side, my family was very nice. My grandmother only spoke Yiddish, and if you couldn't speak Yiddish, you didn't talk to this woman.

My dad, when I was born, had just started working for the outfit in Chicago. I have to tell you this man weighed, in his prime, 385 pounds, and he moved like a cat. I'll even give you a picture if you want. He was big and bad. In fact, my father's family was wild all the way back for eons.

They were considered gypsies in Russia. It wasn't until many years later that I found out Jewish gypsies were the *hondlers*, the people who got things done—if you needed fake papers or someone beat up. That's what they did for hundreds and hundreds of years.

My dad was third man in charge of gambling run by the Jews for the outfit. When I was old enough—six or seven, I mean—he loved to take me to work with him. He'd sit me in front in the cigar store, or I'd be playing around with the guys in the back room who ran the wires. I used to go eat lunch at a local restaurant with all the policemen and the gangsters. When I was ten years old, I was selling rubbers and eight-pagers, the little cartoon dirty books.

My dad had another interesting job with the mob. He was the one who took the money to pay off the police and the judges. When I was seven or eight, he'd put the envelope in my pocket, grab my hand, and we'd go down to City Hall. We'd walk into a courtroom, and he'd stand in the back and wave at the bailiff. The bailiff would come running over. He'd pick me up and throw me around, and I'd hand him the envelope with the money. I can't tell you how many times I did that when I was growing up. And my dad just thought that was the best.

Naturally, there's bad with the good. I saw my father many, many times just knock the shit out of people. And I would get scared out of my mind. All the fights I saw, he was like a maniac.

Here's the advice I got in life from my dad. "You're only guilty if you get caught. Never admit it, and never put it in writing." "Don't ever let anyone get the drop on you." "Always be ready with a story." On my mother's side, I always had this "Be a nice person. Be religious."

My dad was always great to me. As long as I didn't do anything stupid. He could not tolerate stupidity. A couple of times I got arrested, and he'd get mad at me and have to come get me out of jail. Because I was always fighting. Grammar school, high school, it didn't matter.

When I was twelve, I was as big as I am now. I never grew. I was always just a rough, skinny kid. I sort of wore my Jewishness as a chip on my shoulder. If you wanted to fuck around with me, I'd get you. I cannot tell you how many times I got into fights because I was Jewish. Umpteen zillion of them.

I started to get sick with Crohn's Disease at the end of my junior year of high school. Nobody knew what I had. I'd get giant hives, sweating, sleepless nights. My whole body would just go through this horrible thing, and they didn't understand it. I couldn't run track anymore. All I could do on the football team was kick extra points. I didn't have any more strength. And I had been a real gifted athlete.

My mother moved us in my junior year from the west side of town where I was captain of the track team, co-captain of the football team, and, for my age, the fastest kid in the country.

In the new neighborhood, I was living with kids who had little buckles on the back of their pants, and light buck shoes, and crew cuts, and they wore madras shirts. They looked real smart. And I'm up off the west side of Chicago, and here I am with all these people. I didn't belong. I felt out of place.

I graduated high school in '57. I was a very poor student, very poor. My grammar and my English sucks. Who wanted to learn about this bullshit? I always learned from my father, "Just do enough so you pass and I don't have to hear about it, will ya?" I spent my life getting C's through high school and college. That's all I worried about, getting a C. But I knew I had to go to college.

It was a real problem getting into college because my grades were so bad. As a matter of fact, one time in high school I had thirty-two detentions. Well, when you get to thirty-three detentions, you go to reform school. You're supposed to be an incorrigible at this point. And I *wasn't* incorrigible. But I loved joking around, playing games, and maybe I would walk up and smack some guy in the face, that too. I got real close to going to reform school.

I would do anything on a dare. Break that window? Bang! Broken window. I thought I was like my father. Physically, I wasn't there, I wasn't his size, but I had the same mentality.

So I got into college, and after three semesters, I was on probation, on my way out. I was real sick with the Crohn's, too, but no one knew what was wrong with me yet. And when I walked into my first class, and the guy said read the first three chapters and do all the questions in the back, I about had a heart attack. It was a miracle I graduated. I just made it out with a 2.0 in my major.

I went from college to work for the IRS. I sent them a letter and said, "Please hire me." All the accounting firms that came in to interview at the school saw my grades and said, "Next!" But when I got in the IRS, they loved me.

Not because I was book smart, but because I understood what was happening in the streets. After six months of training, they put me in a "super group" as a field agent. Working on large, unusual cases. So there I was at twenty-two years old with an IRS pocket commission.

Six years later, an opportunity came up where I could move to Michigan and buy this small accounting practice. I decided I wanted to try it on my own. Everyone in my family thought it was a great idea to get Stefan out of Chicago. Because even when I was an IRS agent, I was a maniac. I used to run around all night. Doing normal things never made sense to me.

My first tax season, I knew some people who owned bowling alleys, and I set up a card table there with forms. I was doing tax returns in bowling alleys for five dollars a crack.

But the business has always been very good to me. As soon as people knew where my head was, how I thought and how I operated, I was okay. If I'm doing something for you, I'm going to the wall for you. That's how you have to do business in today's world.

Crohn's Disease has pulled me down a lot financially. Over the years, there have been months where I couldn't work. And I'm only making money when my pencil is moving or my mouth is going. That's the bottom line. I have diarrhea every day—the question is when. The less I eat, the less diarrhea I get. But if I don't eat, I could get real skinny and die, so it's a vicious circle.

Basically, Crohn's is an auto-immune disease. It manifests itself primarily in your intestinal tract. Mine's in my ilium. I've had five major surgeries, four minor surgeries. I've had half my intestines out. Two-thirds of my stomach is gone. I've taken medications practically all my life. Hospital stories? I got ten thousand of them.

I've been through many, many experiments with the disease, starting in 1961 at the University of Chicago, where they first diagnosed it. Most doctors had never heard of Crohn's back then. People even told me, "It's all in your head."

By the time I was an IRS agent, everyone knew what was wrong with me. But no one knew how to treat me, except to lay me in bed, put an IV in me, and make me rest. Boy, that's stupid. That don't go.

Crohn's has a lot to do with emotions and trauma, and I am an emotional person, so it's gotten worse over the years. Looking back, my whole life has gone back and forth between the criminal influence from my dad and my desire to be like everybody else. I have always been under this stress. I felt I had to do good, but I didn't have the background, given my family. I was out there slugging it out on my own. After every divorce, I wound up in the hospital with surgery.

My first wife, Joy, I married her in Chicago and we moved here, but she hated it here, so we got separated, and I ended up in the hospital with surgery in '70. Then I married Myra. She was a pledge princess and a May Queen, gorgeous and ya-da-da, ya-da-da... That marriage lasted eight-and-a-half years. After that one, bang! I'm in the hospital, surgery again.

And then my last girlfriend in college calls me up twenty years later. "Stefan, what are you doing? I want to see you." Well, bingo, bango, bungo! She was basically separated from her husband at that point. I did the knight on the white horse driving into town and swooping her up and charging away. She was beautiful, but what I didn't realize was that she was nuts. Anyhow, we got married, and then I got sick again.

Surgery after surgery. Well, that killed the relationship. We broke up, got back together again, then broke up for good. But when she moved out the last time, I got better. Dramatically better. The pain was suddenly gone. The stress was gone. I started seeing there was a pattern, a connection between my illness and my relationships with women. What happened was I figured out that I was basically codependent, and that had a tremendous effect on my life.

Back when I was in my late twenties, I read a book called *Why Am I Afraid To Tell You Who I Am?* It was an eyeopener. I said, "Yeah, I can't tell anybody who I really am." I could be a lot of things—the goofball, the maniac, whatever. I loved all that stuff. But you can't know who I really am. My dad's the gangster. My mother's the perfect little Jewish lady. I don't think I even knew who I was.

What's right and what's wrong? I was always trying to figure that out. And I always tried to emulate my father, always tried to have this deadly toughness in my character. I had his perfect gangster mentality, too, which you have to understand includes taking care of everybody, making sure this person is nice to that person, making sure the money is divvied up right, taking care of the women and children, not lying or messing around with someone else's woman.

Then, I remember, *Jonathan Livingston Seagull* came along. When I read that book, I said, "I think I can understand Jonathan." You have to understand that you're free. It's a hard concept. It really is a hard concept. I was still in relationships, taking care of everybody, running around making sure everything was right for everybody. But I liked that "free" concept.

When my last marriage broke up in '83, I started talking with this client of mine who's a psychologist. She gave me the book *Codependent No More*. Well, I studied it, and I listened to it, and I restudied it. My client said, "Stefan, you're Mr. Codependent, and you're a bad picker."

I said, "You got it, honey. I'm a bad picker. No doubt about it." After studying that book and talking with her a few times, I realized that when you're codependent, you deny yourself the ability to live and enjoy yourself because you're all caught up in other people's crazy nonsense. You get manipulative yourself, trying to keep everything cool.

After figuring out the codependency stuff, I seemed to get my life under control. I started listening to what people were saying about me. We may know six hundred people, for example, 595 who like us and five who don't. And we tend to spend ninety-five percent of our energy on those five jerks and forget about the other 595. That's not smart. I let go of all the negativity, and of the negative people in my life. What a genius! I was only forty-five when I figured this one out. Not bad, huh?

I took one year off from dating. No dating. I didn't want any woman in my life for one year. I bought this house up here on the lake and started fixing it up. I decided to do things I wanted to do. I went fishing. I played with my dogs. I started to paint. It was wonderful.

I began to feel that I was free to live my life. I realized that I didn't have to take care of all these women in my past, or my neurotic mother, or my crazy brother. I could take care of myself.

I discovered that I enjoy living alone. Look where I live. This house is like a chalet in the Alps. I designed this place so that there are no walls surrounding me. It's mostly windows, so it's like living in the open. My backyard is 75 thousand square acres of a beautiful lake.

Even though I was a city kid, I had spent summers up north on the lakes because I had asthma and hay fever. I got into fishing up there. And now I'm back into fishing. Just about every day when I come home from work, I run out back and catch a bunch of fish for dinner. I've learned something about fishing. A fish isn't going to holler at me. He's not going to bite me or make me feel bad. And I love the contest between me and the fish.

Tonight I was the only one out there fishing. What more could a guy ask for? It gives me peace. You see all kinds of things out there, like a king-fisher swooping in to grab a fish, blue herons honking and screaming about their territory, great white egrets fishing along the banks. There's nothing prettier than seeing a four-foot egret walking through the water, stepping real slow, and you know he's going to pop down suddenly for a fish. That's real!

Something else I've learned to enjoy in the last few years—painting. I wondered if I could do it. I don't know all the technical stuff. I'm not really an artist, but I have a good eye for stuff. I got Bob Ross's tapes and books. I watch him do a painting, and I try to do it along with him.

At the end, I look at the painting, and it looks like something. Far out! It's more than a challenge, it's a responsibility. It's about taking care of myself. With me and my disease and my gut, I need to take care of myself.

The painting takes me to another level, a level that's safe, plus I get to make something that's beautiful. I just got done with forty-six paintings, and I raised $4,600 for the Gastro-Intestinal Research Foundation by selling them at $100 a crack. So I get to do something good with the painting, too.

Another thing that's related to the codependency. In '82 and '83, I spent one year in the hospital on my back—for two months at a time, one month at a time—but over a two-year period, if you added it all up, I was on my back fifty percent of the time. I was having chronic diarrhea, too, and I realized that codeine could stop my diarrhea.

I started off taking a Tylenol 3 before dinner, and that was great. This was back in '84. Come '85, maybe I needed, oh, four or five pills a day. In '86, maybe a few more. It was all prescription.

Well, in '91 I started going through a lot of serious dental work, like implants, because I've taken so much Prednisone over the years that it destroyed my teeth. And the doctors were giving me all the codeine I wanted. I was up to twelve Tylenol 4's a day. That's sixty milligrams, a bunch of codeine.

Over the next ten-to-twelve-month period, I got to a point where I was taking forty Tylenol 4's in a twenty-four-hour period. I was taking more codeine, and I was getting sicker. My diarrhea was getting worse, not better. One Saturday afternoon, I took nine at one time. Never felt it. That scared me. I called up a psychologist friend and told her that I was scared and didn't know what to do.

She said, "You have no choice. You've got to go see an addiction specialist over at the hospital." I walked in, and I told the doctor my story. He said, "My God, how long have you been doing this? You should have been in here several years ago."

So I checked myself in with all the drunks and druggies and the rest of the poor souls. I was no different than the rest of them. I fit right in. I realized in that hospital what an obsessive-compulsive personality I have.

About the third or fourth day, we were all in this smoking room on a break from some class, about thirty of us, just puffing away. There was this big ion filter for the smoke and this horrible smell. I was puffing away like a maniac, and I looked around, and I thought, "I'm part of this." Major eye-opener. I realized I had this addictive behavior, and that it was like the codependency. I have to be careful with drugs, people, even caffeine.

I hadn't been able to stop taking the codeine before then. It was like a lifeline—but it had turned into a nightmare. I was scared because I didn't know where I would be at the end of the treatment. But I knew I had to get it together. I knew I couldn't walk out of treatment still messed up. So I stuck it out.

Since I walked out of the hospital on July 12 of last year, I've been clean. And I feel great. I have to tell you, nothing works better than your body on its own. Period.

I go work out at the gym almost every day, and I've never felt so good. All the drugs and all the bullshit's out of my system. I take Imodium for the diarrhea, I take a little bit of Elavil to slow down and quiet my intestinal tract, so I can sleep. That's it. I'm calmer now than when I was in my twenties.

Today, I'm fifty-five years old, and I'm on top of the world. I'm the luckiest guy—I'm alive. I'm the luckiest guy—I'm not in prison. I'm the luckiest guy—I don't have a hole in my head. I have a very nice accounting practice. Rich I'll never be, so I don't worry about that part.

Dating and girls have never really been a problem, as long as I can find someone to meet. I'm dating someone now, but I am not making myself crazy trying to make sure it works for her. I'm not into that codependent crap anymore.

Every once in a while, I party with friends. I hang out. I do what I want to do. And I enjoy living single. It doesn't bother me. It absolutely does not bother me that tonight I will be alone after you leave. I cherish it.

I've created a sanctuary here on the lake. It's a place I can be obsessive and compulsive, but never stupid. The fishing is compulsive—I can't wait to get my line in the water to see what I catch. But it's a good compulsion.

I have to sit back and understand and keep my life in focus. This environment helps me do that. Albert Einstein said the answer is always in the details, and that's an absolute fact. You have to keep it together, focus on the details, be observant about what you're doing. The worst thing in my life right now is accounts receivable, and that ain't so bad.

You know, Jewish people, we don't so much have a heaven or a hell. Our memorial to the future is how we live on in the hearts of those we knew while we were on earth. And that real emotional feeling within a live person—to be carried forward for centuries, even if it is just a little bit—is beautiful. I like that thought.

That's why the heart, trying to do the right thing, is so important to me. To be carried forward in somebody's heart tells me I've truly lived. And I have no responsibilities other than to be a good person, to make my heart feel good.

I'm a happy guy. I really am. Because anything else is stupid.

Talking About It

Ernie Franklin

> I see so many people who are scared to death when you
> say "change." I see the fear on their faces. But if you don't
> change, you're in trouble. Change isn't good in itself—it
> has to have a meaning. But still you have to be able to
> accept it. You shouldn't be afraid of it.

*Ernie Franklin, forty-three years old, comes from a Southern family with a
strong work ethic and traditional ideas about the roles of men and women
in marriage. Not until he was divorced at thirty-one did he begin to question
these assumptions.*

*His questions made him explore the legitimacy of expressing his emotions,
both positive and negative. He also began to consider the necessity
for having fun in life. Good friends supported Ernie in his exploration and
formation of a new self throughout his thirties. In the process of learning to
communicate with and trust in friends, Ernie became more confident and
accepting of life change.*

*Most recently, Ernie has applied his self-reflective skills and acknowl-
edged need to grow to make a significant occupational change: he has left
the ranks of union members and joined management. As a print foreman
at a daily newspaper press, Ernie is enjoying the opportunity to learn new
skills in dealing with people and putting a newspaper on the street.*

*Ernie is a slender man about five-foot-eight, with direct blue eyes and a
wavy mop of brown hair that falls over his forehead. He is dressed in a blue
plaid sports shirt, jeans, and well-broken-in cowboy boots. He has a low,
resonant voice, lightly colored by a Southern accent. We interview him in
the front room of his small but comfortable house, which is decorated with
wooden figures of people and animals, whittled by his father over the years.*

I was fortunate when I was growing up to have known my great-grand-
parents. I remember going to their houses in Tennessee when I was
a child. Grandma and Grandpa Franklin, on my dad's side, had the neatest white house with a big front porch painted gray, and there was this
huge rocking chair on the porch. The house smelled good, and I enjoyed

playing over there. My mom's grandmother, she spent a lot of time with us, too. I still have a picture someone took of us together.

I learned later on that my parents hadn't had an easy time growing up. They had been dirt poor, and they had both worked hard. It makes me appreciate their strength and determination to make something out of their lives. Anything they have, they earned it. I think that probably is the most important lesson I've been taught in my life. If you want anything, you're going to have to earn it. It's not going to be handed to you.

My relationship with my two brothers growing up was typical, I guess. We fought a lot. But I think we loved each other, respected each other. Each of us has a different way of looking at life and a different way of expressing himself. My way was to try to be logical. Sometimes I overevaluated situations. I thought about things a lot before I did them.

I've learned over the years to become comfortable with my first reaction to certain things. I don't second-guess myself as much as I did when I was younger. I think that's a natural part of growing older. That, and being more at home with my decisions.

All of us boys inherited a strong work ethic from our parents. When I was twelve years old, I took a paper route, and I worked almost four years delivering newspapers after school. By the time I was 16, I'd done all right. I mowed lawns, too.

I decided it was time for me to buy a car. I was working at Burger Chef then and making a dollar an hour. I remember exactly what the car cost—$375. A '59 Chevy. When I handed that guy that $375, I felt every dime of it because I had earned it. That was a lot of money in '67.

I think early on, probably in junior high school, I realized that I didn't want to go on to college. Now, looking back, I think I'm just one out of a hundred million who say, "I wish I'd done it different." But at the time, I believed that if I was going to make a living, I was going to have to do it with my hands more than with my brains.

When I got to high school, I took up printing. I had a teacher who gave me the opportunity to go beyond just the basic shop class. Little by little, I got him to show me how they printed stuff. I got so I could run the press pretty good. I stayed with the class through high school.

The more I ran the press, the more I realized that I liked it. I liked starting out with paper and type and finally coming out with a printed product. I ended up majoring in printing in high school. When I graduated from high school, I went to work at the daily newspaper. The older guys took me in right away and showed me the ropes.

The longer I've stayed at the paper, the more education I've received. I guess I knew when I first started to work there that I wanted to move up some day. I was there about four years when an apprenticeship opportunity opened up. I was one of the youngest apprentices they'd ever had. Then I realized I wanted my journeyman's card and maybe a little bit more than that.

When I moved upstairs with the apprenticeship, I got to see more of what went on with the press. I learned by watching various people. If I saw somebody react a certain way in a particular situation, I wondered whether I would react the same way, or would I come at it from a different direction. And I got to see how union representatives—we call them "chapel chairmen"—handled certain situations and people.

This apprentice experience gave me some good insights, I think. It made me look at myself a little bit harder. Up to that point, the only thing that had been important to me was going to work. I had money in my pocket, and everything was pretty good.

I got married in 1972 when I was twenty-one. That changed me a lot. Because it wasn't just me anymore. The money wasn't just for fixing up my car and going out. Two years later, my first son was born, and then it was me and her and this little person. And this little person demanded a lot of time, a whole lot of time. My daughter was born in '76. Then, three years later, we had another boy.

The baby, Rickie, was two years old when we got a divorce. He really didn't understand. He didn't know what was going on, and I couldn't explain it to him. Danny and Tiffany, they were big enough, they knew the word—although I'm not sure they knew what it meant. They just knew I wasn't around all the time anymore.

I had a hard time with the divorce in the beginning. I thought my ex-wife would wake up and realize she had made a mistake and decide that we should get back together. She was the one who initiated the divorce.

Things had not been good for some time before we divorced. We didn't communicate much, talk about what was on our minds, talk about how we felt. We had been like brother and sister for quite some time, instead of like husband and wife. I guess my way of handling trouble was "If I ignore it, it will go away."

Of course, I've learned differently, and I've grown through that. Now I realize that if there's a problem, it needs to be talked about honestly. It needs to be brought out in the open. No beating around the bush.

As we were getting ready to go through our divorce, I started wanting to talk. I wanted to hear what she had to say, too. She brought up stuff that she had held inside her for ten or eleven years. That's a long time to hold something inside. She brought up all kinds of stuff, like, when Danny was born, all the other mothers in the hospital got flowers. I didn't send her any flowers.

I was twenty-three years old when Danny was born. No one had ever told me about what was expected. I had to learn that things like flowers when a child is born, on birthdays, on anniversaries—these things are important.

She talked about a miscarriage she had had. We really hadn't discussed it when it happened, and she asked me when we were getting the divorce why I had never said anything, or why I had never tried to comfort her, why I had had this face of stone, so to speak.

I told her I had been concerned with her health and losing the child, but that I had also been playing my role. I was the husband. I was the strong one. My knees don't buckle. I don't shed tears. Sure, inside I wondered and had questions, but I didn't think I was supposed to show my emotions. I was supposed to keep it all inside me.

The divorce, when I was thirty-one, was a major change. Going from a house full of people to an apartment all alone. I had never lived in an apartment. It could have been the Taj Mahal, I think, and it would still have been the most depressing place I'd ever been in. I hated going in there. Hated it.

I went through a lot of emotions, feelings, thoughts. I had to learn to like myself again. At first, I was second-guessing a lot of stuff. "If I had done this different..." "If I had said this different..." "If I had been more attentive..." Whatever. You just don't know. It just keeps going on in your mind. It drives you nuts.

My ex was very generous as far as letting me see my children. Basically, what I did for two years after the divorce was put my life on hold and spend all my time with my children. I lived my life through them for a while. At the time, I needed that.

A couple of years after the divorce, though, I started to become real good friends with a guy from work. Then Jim invited me to go boating with him and his wife, Patty. And something happened between me and his wife when we met. We just kind of clicked. To this day, I tell everybody she's my best friend. A lot of people may not understand that, but I feel that you can have female friends and that's what they are—female *friends*. She can read me better than I can read myself.

It's a wonder that Jim and Patty didn't beat me and run me out of town, I talked so much to them about the divorce, about my feelings, about the kids. They weren't judgmental. They would just sit there and listen. I credit them with helping me hang on to what little sanity I still had at the time. And I credit them with teaching me how to laugh again, and have fun, and realize I'm a person who deserves to be happy.

Every once in a while when I went somewhere with my friends, at first I'd feel guilty, I'd find myself laughing or joking or having a good time, and suddenly I'd say, "Wait a minute. I'm here by myself. My kids should be here. My wife should be here." It took me a while to get to the point where I knew I was entitled to enjoy my life.

I don't want to sound like I was happy about getting a divorce, but the fact is it opened up a whole new world for me. It gave me an opportunity to expand myself, to take a real hard look at what I wanted and where I wanted to be. I didn't want the divorce, but I grew tremendously as a result of the experience.

In 1986, I decided to buy a house again. I looked at a lot of different places; then a house came up for sale down the street from Jim and Patty. I asked them what they thought about me being so close. They had no problems with it, and over the years, it has worked out.

I'm very comfortable with my house. I've realized how much I enjoy having a place I can call my own, how much I enjoy puttering around and fixing things up.

About a year and a half ago, I took a foreman's job that has meant a major change at this point in my life. It meant joining management and leaving the union. I did a lot of self-evaluation when I applied for the job. I'd been working at the newspaper for about twenty-five years.

When I came out of my apprenticeship, I took a union-representative job. After that, I became the vice president, then president of the local printing pressmen's union. Basically, I've had every union position at one time or another. That was important because it gave me an opportunity to learn what's involved in working with people.

I've been involved in several contract negotiations over the years. The last time I was trying to convince the membership to propose that the employer contribution to the retirement fund be changed from a set dollar amount to a percentage. Some people didn't agree with me. They couldn't see the benefit of a percentage contribution.

That made me look real hard at some of the men I was working with. When I was younger, I thought that they were sharp, that they really knew what was going on. These guys were like my heroes.

That contract situation, and other union experiences, have made me realize I have to start thinking for myself, thinking about what is best for me. These experiences have also made me realize that I'm not as dumb as I thought I was because I didn't have more education.

Moving from being a union man to being a foreman is a big jump. Some people look at me as if I'm the enemy now. But I thought I had done everything I could for the union, and I don't feel like I've had to compromise myself in order to hold the job. I told management I was not going to be a "yes" person, and they said they wanted me anyway.

I talked the job over with my mom and dad. My dad was always one of the workers, a real union man, but he thought I should do what I thought was best for me. Taking the foreman's job put some strain on my relationship with Jim at first, but he never pressured me not to take the job. Still, we don't talk about work as much as we used to. We both agreed it would be best if we didn't.

Some of the guys feel like Jim shouldn't have anything to do with me anymore. Sometimes they break their necks to get to Jim, to tell him what they think I'm up to. That bothers me. I wish they would leave him alone.

I avoid Jim pretty much at work, but he and I still talk and socialize just as much outside the shop. We travel and get together on the weekends. I think our friendship is still as strong as it was.

As far as the foremanship itself goes, I felt like I needed a change in my life. And that has happened. One of the first things I found out I would have to change is my wardrobe. I'm comfortable in jeans and clothes along those lines, but I found that when I'm dealing with people from the upper floors, maybe bluejeans isn't the right attire. Now I have Dockers and a couple of corduroy sportscoats. I think my tie selection has increased, too!

I just had my first education seminar here about a week ago concerning sexual harassment. It was an eye-opener. I've also had an opportunity to learn more about the newspaper. Recently, I sat in on a deadline meeting and listened to different department heads talk about their jobs. It gives me a lot better appreciation of what other people have to do to put 180 thousand papers out on the street every day.

I feel real confident about taking on this new role. I feel secure because of what I've been through on my job. I don't want to get stagnant again. If somebody comes up to me and starts talking about a subject I don't know anything about, I want to be able to go out and learn about it, so I can come back and continue with the conversation. I want to be able to continue to grow until the day they put me in the ground.

I'm pretty happy with where I am personally, too. I've been divorced twelve years now. I'm self-sufficient. I can dress myself! And wash clothes. And cook a little. Maybe someday, I'll get married again. I don't want to grow old by myself. I'd like to have somebody around. I try to keep my options open.

It's harder for a man to learn to do more than just work. It's like you're not supposed to have fun. Or show emotions. No matter how hard you want to cry, you know you're not supposed to. But crying is an honest emotion, and if you're sad, you should cry.

Maybe I learned that late in life, but I did learn it. And I have to talk about it. I can't just ignore it and push it to the side anymore. Communication is important.

I see so many people who are scared to death when you say "change." I see the fear on their faces. But if you don't change, you're in trouble. Change isn't good in itself—it has to have a meaning. But still, you have to be able to accept it. You shouldn't be afraid of it.

Super Big, Super Tough

Zach Wolfe

> That first visit to the psychiatrist was one of the hardest
> things I'd ever done, because I had to admit defeat. I'm
> very competitive, and I hate to admit defeat. I had tried
> out for the Green Bay Packers. I was tough! I was captain
> of the football team in college. I held the school record
> in the shotput in college. I was one of the outstanding
> seniors. I was all right. I did not want to admit defeat,
> and it was a real blow to me, to my ego. I was ashamed,
> really ashamed.

*The heroic image of the football player has played a large part in the
mythology of the American male. Coaches' directives to work hard, be
tough, and endure pain are messages about being a man. Such lessons
require men to sacrifice other needs and feelings in order to maintain their
role as team players. But the promise of glory earned on the gridiron is not
always forthcoming in the real world.*

*Zach Wolfe, a fifty-five-year-old retired high school teacher and coach,
understands all too well the long-term effects of being strong, silent, and
long-suffering. Although his hair is almost completely white now, his six-
foot-two frame is still a powerful physical reminder of his earlier aspiration
to a career in football.*

*Despite Zach's size, one is immediately aware of his gentleness. He is a quiet
man with a warm, boyish grin, a genuine and caring person. But his sports-
manlike commitment to go the limit to help others contributed to a bout with
depression in his early fifties. Like so many men, Zach had carried around
unexpressed feelings of frustration and hurt—feelings typically denied to
men—until he could no longer cope.*

*In counseling, Zach began the process of changing the overdeveloped sense
of responsibility and competitiveness that had led him to a midlife breakdown.
He learned the importance of self-care and the simple value of just being,
rather than doing. Discovering joy in creative pursuits and simple pleasures
has also been part of his healing process. He says about the woodworking he
now enjoys, "I learned the love of it from my father."*

Zach has been successful in making changes in his professional life; his challenge now is to create the same balance in his personal life. Spending time with family and friends, as well as taking time for fishing trips and hobbies, hold him to his new direction.

He still lives in the small town where he was born and raised. We go to dinner with Zach and his wife, Alice, at an Italian restaurant that had been a favorite after-prom hangout in their high school years. Later, we tour their small backyard and talk about the garden. It is early spring. A pile of cherry wood nestles against the side of the garage waiting for Zach to transform it into the tables, bookcases, and clocks he makes as gifts for family and friends.

I enjoyed childhood. We weren't rich, but I didn't realize it. I enjoyed everything. I liked to read. My favorite afternoons in summer were when the sun was bright. I would get a little bit of money and buy a quart of rootbeer and a pint of ice cream and make rootbeer floats and read.

My mother used to read to us. She gave my brother and sister and me the joy of reading. My parents had lots of books around, and I went to the library all the time.

When I was little, my dad worked at the steel works, and after eighteen years of that, he came home one day and said he had quit. He had an ulcer and arthritis, and he couldn't take the stress. He became a carpenter then and had a business most of his life after that. And that was shaky financially. He went bankrupt when I was a junior in high school.

My father influenced me a lot. He never said a whole lot. We never had any heart-to-heart talks. But I learned by just being around him, seeing what he did and how he acted, by working with him when I was in high school, by seeing him go to work every day even though he had arthritis and an ulcer. He was always a hard worker. He never complained, never missed a day of work unless he was sick in bed.

My father set the tone for me. I learned that you don't give up and that, no matter what happens, you do what you have to without complaining. I learned the work ethic from him, and also from sports. That was good and bad. It did hurt me at times. I didn't know when to lay off, when to stop. I think that led to the breakdown I had later as a teacher.

My mother was an influence, too. She gave us values. She taught us to be fair, to be honest, to respect other people. She had a high regard for education. She was an honor student in high school, and she never got to go to college. And she regretted that for the rest of her life. She really wanted us to go to college.

I was insecure in school. I thought everybody else was smarter than I was. I would sit in back of the class, afraid to ask questions because I thought everybody else knew the answers. I was afraid I'd look stupid if I asked a question. It was only in graduate school that I learned that I had just as much ability as everybody else. That kind of bothers me now, that nobody ever encouraged me. Because I just floated through high school. I didn't realize how much more I could do.

I really enjoyed sports as a kid. It was just the thing to do, to go out and play some kind of ball with my friends. We didn't have television, so I just went out and played sports all the time. Sports became a big thing in my life. A real big thing.

I enjoyed being around the guys I played football with in high school—the attitude, the enthusiasm, the spirit. I never got really close with any of the guys. But we did things together. We enjoyed each other. We talked a little bit, although I never really opened up. I never shared any of my dreams or secrets. I was always a listener. And a follower, probably.

But I enjoyed the association. And I enjoyed the physical part of it, you know, pushing yourself, working hard, developing your body and feeling good about it. I enjoyed competing against other guys. Beating them. Winning. I was very competitive.

I became a teacher because of athletics. The coaches had been the important people in my life, the important influences. They had instilled in me the attitude of winning and the love of competition. They had had a positive attitude. They taught that you, not somebody else, determine what you do in life. Originally, I majored in business in college, then decided it wasn't for me and decided to become a teacher and a coach.

My wife and I started going together in my junior year in high school. We got married between semesters in my junior year in college. Our oldest son was born a month after I graduated from college. That was five days before I left for a tryout with the Green Bay Packers.

I was in Green Bay about three weeks, and it was a good experience as I look back on it. Being a small part of something great. Getting to know Vince Lombardi and Bart Starr. It gave me bragging rights.

But it was very, very competitive, and so cutthroat. These guys who were trying out were the cream of the crop. You had to be super fast, super big, super tough. I was tough enough, I think, but I wasn't fast enough.

I wasn't disappointed when I didn't make it, not really, not once I got there and saw the talent level of all the other guys. There were two spots open, and there were fifty rookies. So I had to be one of two out of those fifty. You had to be a superstar just to make the team.

I was twenty-one when I started teaching. My first year, I made $4,200. Take-home pay was $126 for two weeks. We couldn't live on it. I resigned at the end of the year so I could try out for the Buffalo Bills. I didn't make the team, so I came home and got another teaching job.

In addition to teaching that next year, I played in an area pro team. I taught during the day, had practice every evening, and played every weekend. We won two out of fourteen games that season. I got fifty dollars a game. It was enough to buy a new washer and dryer that year. The coaching was poor and everything was disorganized, so I decided to quit.

After that, besides teaching, I always had two or three part-time jobs going to keep our heads above water. I was an insurance investigator for three years. I painted houses in the summer. I was a fireman for three summers. I did carpentry work and had my own floor-sanding and -finishing business going for seven years. I was working on my master's degree when the school system where I was working offered me a job in Special Education. I decided I'd try it.

About my twelfth year of teaching Special Ed—in my mid-thirties, I guess—I was offered a job in New South Wales, Australia, in a little country school two hundred miles inland. It took us three months to get through the culture shock. It was a slow pace of life. An Australian colloquialism is "Not to worry, mate. She be right." So everything moved very slowly. We didn't have a telephone. Didn't have a TV for six months. We thought life would be very much the same, you know, but it was a totally different culture.

People were more important to one another over there. They didn't have a lot of possessions, and they didn't worry about it. There were no class distinctions between people. The hospital administrator, the banker, the principal, the teachers, the farmers—everyone got along fine and helped each other out. Instead of going their separate ways on the weekend, everybody got together for picnics and dinners and parties and outings.

When we came home a year later, it was hard to adjust. Life here seemed so impersonal, so fast and so fake, people all rushing around trying to keep up with everybody else. Our values had changed in Australia. People had become more important to us. Family had become more important than worrying about getting a new car or a new house. I'd rather spend money visiting friends than buying things. Image is not important to me. We drive a car till it's ready for the junkyard.

When I was forty-five or forty-six, I injured my back at a winter camp program for sixth graders. I was in the hospital for nine days. The school system refused to honor the Workman's Comp claim, and I had to get a lawyer and fight to get the bills paid. That's how the school system treated teachers.

I flipped out, really. I told my principal, "Do not ask me to do anything extra. I will not do it. I'm through volunteering." I had volunteered for everything before. I started the ski club, I was faculty manager of all the athletics—for no extra pay. I collected all the money, made sure all the referees were there, got people to supervise on every sporting activity for six years. I went on all the trips. I went to all the dances because I thought it was part of the job, you know? Help the kids and do the most I could. And whatever I did, the administration would want more.

In the back of my mind, I think I probably felt that if you work hard enough you're going to get advanced, get a better position. At least get some recognition, some thanks.

I was very, very hurt by the school system's response to my injury. It was totally devastating. I didn't want to teach after that. I told the principal I was going to do as little as possible. But that bothered me, too. Because that went against everything I'd always stood for. So I was stuck in the middle. I didn't want to volunteer, but I didn't want to hurt the kids.

A year later, I had my breakdown. For the six or seven years before the breakdown, I was frustrated because there was no feedback from the administration. Almost no appreciation from parents. There were no positive strokes.

No matter what you did, if you did it well, you stayed there, and they added to it. If you could handle more, you got more. No extra pay. And even though you did extra duty, you didn't make any more than the person who didn't do anything. That always frustrated me, that you could bust your butt and never make any more money. You could be the best one there and never make any more money.

That got to me. Our kids were getting to college age, and we didn't have any savings—never had any savings. We lived pay-to-pay. I couldn't afford to send my kids to college. They were going to have to find the money somewhere else.

I had felt that I could do anything that I set my mind to do. But because I had chosen teaching, the family was suffering financially. I was so hooked on teaching, I believed in it so much, that I continued even though I felt I was sacrificing my family.

I was getting burned out, really. I was waking up more tired than when I went to bed. I'd wake up in the middle of the night thinking about my students—what can I do with this kid or that kid to motivate him? I was totally exhausted, mentally and physically.

I thought, "I need a change. I've got to get out of this school." So I transferred to elementary school. I went the first day at the beginning of the school year, and I couldn't go back the second day. Nothing special happened that day. It was just a normal day. But I came home, I started crying, and I couldn't stop crying. My heart was racing and pumping, and I had a pain in my chest. I got up the next morning, and I started crying again. I didn't know why. And I couldn't go back.

I called the principal and told him, "I'm not coming back. I don't know if I'll ever be back." I called the personnel director and told him the same thing. He came over—he was a good person—and he said, "Take care of yourself. Here's a psychiatrist I recommend. You gotta get yourself some help, and do it right now. Don't worry about school."

That first visit to the psychiatrist was one of the hardest things I'd ever done, because I had to admit defeat. I'm very competitive, and I hate to admit defeat. I had tried out for the Green Bay Packers. I was tough! I was captain of the football team in college. I held the school record in the shot-put in college. I was one of the outstanding seniors. I was all right! I did not want to admit defeat, and it was a real blow to me, to my ego. I was ashamed, really ashamed.

I was ashamed that I couldn't handle it, ashamed that I wasn't strong enough to take care of things. I had always thought I could take anything—that I could always take another year. I would get depressed during the year, and I would count the days. I'd think, "I've got forty-five days till the end of the year, seven weeks. I can handle that. I can take it. I've got the summer to look forward to." The summer to get well, you know?

But I just got to the point where I couldn't take it anymore. That was hard to admit to myself because I had always felt I could deal with anything.

At first, I couldn't go out in the front yard. I could go out in the back yard because nobody could see me in the back yard. So that was terrible. That was terrible! Gradually, I got to the point where I could go to the grocery store. But I hoped nobody would see me who knew me, and I especially did not want to see any of the kids who were in my class.

One day I was at the grocery store, and here comes this girl who was in the class, way across the market. "Mr. Wolfe, where have you been?" I wanted to shrivel into the floor. I said, "Oh, I've been sick." "Are you coming back?" she asked me. I said, "I don't know. I have to get well first."

But each time I went to the psychiatrist, it got easier. I looked forward to talking to him. I had never talked to anybody like that before, never talked about my feelings to anybody before, never shared my fears, things like that. During that time, my wife was very supportive of anything and everything I did. Just totally behind me, in a quiet way.

Gradually, I came out of it. I started doing a lot of woodworking in my garage. I made all the Christmas presents that year. I made a kitchen table and benches, a big hall clock, a Victorian mirror, and some musical toys. I started having fun. I *really* started having fun—with the woodworking, staying home, reading, cooking, and just watching TV.

After a while, people would ask me why I wasn't teaching, and I would tell them, "I had a breakdown." It kind of floored them that I would be that honest. But I felt that was part of getting better. Don't dodge the problem.

When I went back to work, I had a very good year. The next year I was selected Teacher of the Year, and I have had no problem since. Because I had learned to take care of myself first, not to let those other people affect me. I did my job and did the best I could. I didn't kill myself volunteering. I did the job in class and said the hell with the administration. I needed to take care of myself.

From my talks with the psychiatrist, I also realized that I couldn't save the world. I did what I could for those students, but I couldn't save the world. And with that attitude, I was very successful. I taught two-and-a-half more years until I retired.

Teaching Special Education, you don't see a lot of growth, and that was hard because you never got any closure. There was always something more to do, never a finished product. In painting houses and carpentry work, there's a product. I can see a result and it feels good. I need that. I needed some closure in my life. It wasn't coming from the teaching.

It could have. It could have come from the administration in the form of a "thank you" once in a while. In the form of "Hey, you're doing a good job." That would have been closure. But it didn't happen. Instead, the shit came down all the time.

But even though I've complained about the finances and the problems, I enjoyed teaching, and I was a good teacher. I don't think it's big-headed to say that. I've been an important person in the lives of many kids, and I'm proud of that.

After we came back from Australia, I tried to adopt some of that attitude they have, "Not to worry." And it worked, up to a point. But the more things that happen, the less attainable it is. Since my son-in-law was killed last year, I've realized we're not in control of so many things. Now I worry about everybody around me—our kids, our grandkids, our friends.

There seems to be a fight within me about worrying and not wanting to worry. I just live with it. I pray. Make deals. I know it's kind of meaningless to do that, but I still pray about it.

Woodworking is very satisfying to me now. I think it's an extension of my father. He was a very good carpenter, a very good woodworker. I like to create things in woodworking and stained glass. I don't like to work from diagrams. I just start from scratch, try to picture it and draw it myself and go from there.

It has been very satisfying to work with my hands. It's healing. When I make stuff, I just feel so much better, and I don't worry about other things. I like the smell of the wood and the feel of it. It's enjoyable to use the tools and the machines to come up with a product.

And I'm not a perfectionist at all. It's kind of like the way I like my lifestyle to be, loose and easy, just go with what works. I do things my way, and if there's a little something wrong with it, that's just a part of it. Whereas in teaching I was very competitive, I don't compete with anybody in woodworking or in stained glass. It's just a good, satisfying feeling.

These days, I enjoy my dogs and my grandkids. Someday, I want to go fishing with all five of my grandkids. I figure eight years from now. The youngest will be nine years old. The oldest will be thirteen. I'd like to be an influence in their lives.

Coming Home

Lou DeWein

I think I'm in the process of coming home. I think it was
Carl Jung who wrote about how, when you're young, you
learn who you are relative to your mother and your father
and your social community. Then you become socialized,
and you start moving away from that. And then, at some
point, you either go flying out into space, or you start
pulling home. I think I'm in the pulling home process.

*Niches, a rustic retreat center in Vinton County, Ohio, is the result of the
midlife quest of Lou DeWein (his real name) for more meaningful work.
Lou, a former college professor, began his search following a period of inner
restlessness and career dissatisfaction in his forties. A career counselor was
Lou's guide as he examined, among other things, his childhood and his
current passion for clues to a new vocation.*

*Gradually, Lou began to understand how he had rejected his childhood
roots. His return to rural life is a return to those roots, but Lou's home-
coming is more than a nostalgic retreat to the way things were. Although
his boyhood has been a strong influence in the creation of Niches, it is Lou's
adult commitment to the concepts of ecology, solitude, and community that
lies at the heart of his way of life. Nevertheless, Lou's story provides an
excellent example of how men in midlife can successfully reintegrate interests and themes from their childhood into their adult lives.*

*Lou has a small but muscular build, no doubt a result, in part, of the
physical labor required to keep Niches going. He wears jeans and a grey
T-shirt with the Niches logo. He is an intense, energetic man who speaks
rapidly, as though he is racing to keep up with his thoughts.*

*Lou's living area is quite small. Pictures of his parents sit on a shelf above
an antique gas cooking stove; both pictures and stove are reminders of
simpler times. A wood stove in the corner warms the room on this cold
February day. A colorful hand-painted screen and many Mexican artifacts,
including a weaving on the wall, brighten the room. A computer on Lou's
desk is the only concession to modern life.*

*Niches consists of several small cabins and one larger cabin that sleeps
six in the loft. The only electricity and running water are in Lou's house.*

Each sparsely furnished cabin has a wood stove for heat and kerosene lamps for light. Hammocks hang in the larger cabin, in the picnic pavilion, and throughout the property. They are Niches' signature.

Childhood is real important. I've been thinking about it a lot since I started this process of changing careers. It was one of the major themes of the career counseling I had in midlife.

I was unhappy with my career, and I thought that I was unhappy with life in general, so I went to see a psychotherapist for a couple of sessions. I came to realize through her that I was really in the middle of a career change, or possible change, and, that if I didn't make it, I would become a bitter old person and settle into a job that was no longer satisfying.

The therapist sent me to a career counselor, and for two or three months, we talked about my childhood. And that became very instrumental because so much of my childhood is playing out in this endeavor. I'll be doing work here in the surroundings I've created, and either the work itself or the surroundings will catapult me back in time. I'm having a lot of flashes of childhood.

We lived in Ashtabula County, Ohio. There was a church, a school, my mother and father's house, which became the general store of the community, and the neighbors who farmed, a community of 300 or 400 people.

As I grew up, I enjoyed walking through the woods, and walking through fields, and getting lost in cornfields, and building forts in the barn, and raising every animal in the book. Not as a farming endeavor, but as a kind of a hobby. I had pigs and goats and turkeys and chickens and geese and pet rabbits, and a pet pig that I used to ride.

Something else about my childhood came to me last year. I was going swimming at a nearby camp. I was swimming out to this raft, and I noticed it had a diving board. I kept looking at that diving board and feeling this incredible pull.

It was way up there, and I'm not too cool with heights. I just stood there for the longest time and, all of a sudden, just jumped. And halfway down, I flashed on jumping off of a covered bridge when I was a boy. I didn't know it at the time, but that was my initiation into the big boys' group.

In my community, at about the age of puberty, the younger boys were allowed to start going places with the older boys. And one of the places we were allowed to go with the older boys was swimming. Each of the older boys was sort of assigned to a younger boy.

We would go to this place and everybody would swim, and we would swim naked. It was a real male thing. You got to see the older boys' genitals and start thinking about how you were going to be when you grew up. And you heard them talk about being with girls. So you started that whole process.

But the point when you knew you were one of them was when you would go up to the bridge over the river. It was a covered bridge, and on the side of it some fallen planks had left a hole. And there was this one place in the water, about the size of this room, that you could jump into. If you jumped any other place, you would get hurt because the river was shallow.

The older boys would get on the edges of these rock ledges so you could clearly see where the place to jump was. One day I decided I wanted to jump. This had something to do with becoming a man. It was like you could take the responsibility for your own actions. You had to do it once you started it. You knew you had the support of the other boys, but there was still a risk.

When I jumped off that diving board last year, halfway down I saw those guys on the rocks. I saw the water. I could feel the hole in the bridge behind me. Can you see that I'm doing a lot of flipping into childhood as I tell you this now?

I went to elementary school for the first eight years, a little rural school with maybe six or seven rooms. When ninth grade came, we were shipped to town. We were all psyched about it. The school bus came that first day and picked us all up at the elementary school, where we would meet.

We started getting off the bus, and we heard some city kids saying, "Oh, here come the hicks." It was the first thing I heard as I got off the bus. And it was like a real hard force that came right in. I think that was where I began to deviate away from my roots. Because I bought into it. At some unconscious level, I decided that my roots were no good.

I didn't want to be called a hick. I wanted to look at those kids and be part of their community, you know? Of course, I didn't think about it in quite that way then. So I went about this process of denying my roots and embracing the upper-class high school culture.

In my sophomore year, I started dating a girl from the country club and began the process of becoming someone else. My personality started being molded by other people—her family began to mold me. It became important to me that my family have dinner with a proper table setting. Because my family was, like, no table cloths. We sat down with different kinds of dishes. It was a real struggle for my mother and father to get anything, so this must have been a wrenching time for them. I think they could see me starting to turn my back on what their life was all about.

My girlfriend was going to Ohio State, and so I entered Ohio State. Her family thought I should be a physician. I went down with the idea of going to medical school. I entered the pre-medical curriculum. My girlfriend joined a sorority. I joined a fraternity.

My dad had to get an extra job to support me, and I didn't even appreciate it. It was almost like I had come to expect...you know, that attitude that you have. And I was imitating. Of course, you go to college. Of course, you join a fraternity. Of course, of course.

But because I partied a little too much and did a lot of socializing, I only got a 2.9 grade-point average. And it was—whoa!—devastating. Everything was supposed to fall in line the way my new culture had planned it.

I remember once, during that time, I came home, and I started getting on my mother and father's case about our home. My father raised his hand and just smacked me across my face. He said, "Don't ever belittle your home." It was a real shocker. And a point came where I realized what I had done in terms of moving away from my family.

Shortly after that, I got the rejection from med school. Bells were starting to go off that something was amiss here. But the pattern had been set about what I was supposed to do.

I got the idea that I would go to graduate school for a year and see if I could prove myself to get into med school. But my advisor, a Japanese woman, asked me to continue working on a Ph.D., and her influence at the time was important to me.

When I finished my Ph.D., I was so hungry to get away from everything. I decided I would take the summer off before I started teaching and go to Mexico.

Mexico was just an incredible experience because I had never seen another culture, and I got whipped into a Third-World country...I mean, we were out in the boondocks. I saw Indians living in villages, and boy, it reached into me hard.

One night I went to a little bar in this place called Palenque, which was in this tropical rain forest, and there was a group of archaeologists there from all over the world. They were talking about what was going on in these ruins at Palenque.

I went over and introduced myself. They were passing bottles of liquor around and talking high-level stuff about hieroglyphs and the Mayans. I got royally drunk and fell into the aura of this past culture. History had never meant anything to me before that. I had no history. Because my parents were orphans, we never had that infusion of grandparents' stories, so my life was always present-oriented or future-oriented.

A whole world opened up to me. I just fell into this other culture, and I began to see how cultures come and go. It gave me some perspective on my culture. And the experience in the tropical rain forest just bolted me into ecology.

That was a pivotal time for me. I fell hopelessly in love with Mexico, and I still go back quite a bit. And that plays out here at Niches in the hammocks, and in a lot of the building designs, and in the names of the cabins.

I guess, at that time, I just accepted that I would be a college teacher and get my retirement, and then I would travel and maybe write a book and stuff like that. I'd been teaching physiology at Capitol University about ten or twelve years when it just began to be boring. The same old courses. I was tired of talking to eighteen- and nineteen-year-old minds. I was in my mid-thirties. My agitation began to turn me into...you know, it's like when you're irritated with somebody and you want to just nitpick at them all the time?

I started finding all these faults with the university, and supporting causes, and joining people who were bitching about this or bitching about that. And while the bitching was sometimes legitimate, it was also a convenient way for me to begin to vent my inner dissatisfaction.

Then one day, I just walked out of there. Just quit. I took a teaching position at a college in Pennsylvania. The college was okay and everything, but it was the same job, right? So I got bored again very quickly.

And I had no idea what I was doing in terms of yanking myself out of my social connection in Ohio, just picking up and leaving it and dropping down somewhere where I didn't know anybody. I cried for the first time in my adult life, probably every other night. I was so lonely and so sad. And that was very important because it told me that I really can't trivialize the social connections in my life. Those are very important. When you get them, you keep them.

Eventually, I came back to Columbus and lived with a friend for about three or four months, and my money ran out. This was a shocker for me. Like some kid who was used to getting an allowance all his life, I waited and nothing happened. It was like someone was supposed to offer me a job or something. "My God, I have a Ph.D.!"

At that point, I began to think that I was no longer a professor. I knew I didn't want to be a professor, so I denied that I had a degree and an education and a mind. I didn't know what to do, so I started doing just about anything. I was a nude model for a while at art schools and worked as a trainer with a group of consultants who were using psycho-social drama for learning experiences.

Emotionally, I felt free for the first time in a long time. At the same time, the business of not being able to pay my bills and the business of not having real work was depressing. And my self-confidence dropped low. So it was back and forth—I like it, I don't like it. It goes back to concepts of what work means. I was doing jobs, but the jobs didn't seem to suit a person with a Ph.D. Therefore, I felt trapped.

Back when I was working on my graduate degree, I started coming down to Southern Ohio every weekend. I loved being down here. That was when the country theme started coming back into my life. I continued coming down, pretty much every weekend, all through my teaching career.

I knew in my heart I wanted a piece of land that was mine. I heard about this land that was for sale, and I bought it. There was nothing on it, no driveway, nothing. I cleared a little spot where the parking lot is now, and I would come down and put my tent there—a little Volkswagen and a little tent that looked like the Volkswagen. I would camp down here at least two weekends a month.

I would just walk all around this place, following deer trails. I became intimate with the land. It's like when you get to know people, you hang around them a lot and you start noticing the little creases in their faces or their smells. That's what I did.

Until the discontent started, I was a city person. In addition to the career conflict, I was becoming very uncomfortable in the city, very uncomfortable. I was tired of sitting in traffic lines, you know. I just felt I had to get out of there. It was a real strong drive.

But I felt I was trapped. I thought I was a teacher. I was on a career path. I had tenure. I was an associate professor. It was very difficult to step out of that. I began to get depressed.

When I went to a career counselor, I learned that what was important was to lead a productive life. The counselor told me that she could help me create that according to deep things within me and that we needed to know what made me happy as a person. We needed to know what kind of an environment I needed to be in and what I wanted out of life.

She jumped on the childhood theme first and really did a lot with that. And then she said, "Tell me what you've done in your life." I told her about coming down here to Vinton County, and she said, "That's a pretty strong pull, isn't it?"

We talked for several sessions about what I did when I was down here in the country, why I came down here, what was the draw. I realized that when I came down here, I would automatically feel less stressed. It gave me more time for reflection. Whereas when I was in the city, I was so busy doing the stuff that I do, some of which was just to keep me from getting depressed, I didn't have time for reflection.

What the counselor heard in what I was saying were these nature themes and these community themes. There were so many similarities between coming here and what I had done as a child. After I did some writing exercises and we had talked for a long time, she said, "You have an incredible need for variety in your life. Newness and creativity are very, very important to you."

One day she said something about running a camp or running a retreat center. "A retreat center?" I said. "What do you mean?" She said, "There are different kinds of retreat centers where people go away from their normal lives and do something. That something depends on the retreat."

That sounded interesting. The idea of a retreat center just took over, and I could begin to see it, see people doing things, laying around in hammocks and having delightful conversations and food. And that's the way it's worked out.

Running a retreat center is incredibly satisfying because I've come to realize it's the first time in my life that I'm doing what I want to do and not doing somebody else's agenda, somebody telling me I'm a good technician or I ought to go to medical school. It's the first time I've learned to do something entirely with my own hands for my own self-support. It's like, if it doesn't happen with these two hands, there's no big university parent who is going to pull me out. I'm up to my eyeballs here.

Besides, at this point I'm real interested to see if I can take care of myself. And I chose, also, to do it in a real basic way. I'm responsible for my own water. I'm responsible for my own heat. I'm responsible for a lot of things that I used to pass off on others before, when I made the money and paid the bills. It's some sort of self-sufficiency thing. I think I just felt that I had become an overeducated fool.

Going to Mexico had a lot to do with it. When you see people living close to the earth...well, it jumped me back to my childhood again. Because when my mom and dad moved out to the country, we didn't have running water. We didn't have electricity. We had outhouses. My mother and father had a garden, and they grew the vegetables. And there was something deep in me that wanted to see if I could do it, too. I didn't want so many people between me and the stuff that was bottom-line.

Creating Niches was part of getting out of my head, too. After going to school so long, the cognitive part of my being was developed and well-trained, perhaps because that went well with whatever concept there was in my head about being a man. But I hadn't seen models of men letting their hearts hang out. I was heavily trained cognitively, but not emotionally. And my sensory capacity, I think, had been dulled.

When I came to Niches, other parts of me came around. The sensory input was just overwhelming, like the smells of the place—as opposed to the limited sensory input when I was living in the city. I started noticing that I would often get teary-eyed in response to nature. I didn't understand my reaction. Men don't really know what the word "emotional" means. It's like when we started having wet dreams, when that happens, and we don't know what is happening or what to do about it. But the more I just allowed the feelings to be there, the more my emotional side developed.

When I first moved here, I experienced these episodes of being afraid. At first, I didn't even know what I was afraid of. I would sit in the cabin petrified that a face would appear in the window. One night I was sitting in the chair, looking out the window being afraid, and I said, "You have to go out there and confront it." So I went out, and I was shaking so hard I could hardly stand it, and there was nothing there.

Then this little voice said, "Take a walk. You need to go walking through the woods and test this out." So I walked, and it was the most terrifying, as well as the most edifying, walk I've ever taken. Fear of the dark was something I had dragged out from my childhood. I was afraid of the dark when I was a kid.

But I think the dark was also a metaphor about starting a new path, and I didn't know where I was going, and that was scary. So that opened up the idea that I had a fear of failure, that I would fail and everybody would laugh at me. I didn't want to be ridiculed, and I didn't want to fall flat on my face.

After that walk, I was totally okay. A huge weight lifted off my psyche. I'm really coming to understand that people need a balance between solitude and community. At least I do. I need the time to be introspective and to be alone, to know who I am in relationship to this bigger picture. And I need solitude for my own inner calmness. The part of me that, as a child, went out into the woods to be alone, that part needs to be fed.

I think I'm in the process of coming home. I think it was Carl Jung who wrote about how, when you're young, you learn who you are relative to your mother and your father and your social community. Then you become socialized, and you start moving away from that. And then, at some point, you either go flying out into space, or you start pulling home. I think I'm in the pulling home process.

People ask me a lot if I'm lonely. The answer is no. When the people are gone, it's just wonderful. It's delightful. And that's because of something else that's happened to me about four years ago. It was a very profound experience.

I was walking up to the other little cabin, and it was dusk, and the trees were mostly silhouetted. At one point along the way, the trees kind of approach, really close. As I moved in there, I started feeling really weird, and I looked up, and there was just a tiny red hue on the horizon. The sun had just gone down. And the trees were black.

All of a sudden, I felt like I was falling into a big hole. I remember falling into it and feeling a momentary fear. There were three or four seconds where I felt like I had lost consciousness. I didn't fall down, but I fell into this hole, and when I came out of it, it felt good. I tried to make it happen again, but I couldn't. So I went around doing my business, but it bothered me because I thought maybe I had had a stroke. I'm fifty-three. Why else would I black out?

Then, maybe four weeks later, it happened again. I was about ready to go see a physician when somebody sent me an article on a subject called "deep ecology," which is a philosophical consideration of ways different cultures view ecosystems.

So I'm reading along, and I come to something called the "ecological self." And it says that lots of times, when people begin this journey of getting to know a piece of land intimately, they lose the separation between themselves and the rest of the living world. There's like this skin that you have, and it begins to weaken, and your identity starts becoming that place, as well as who you are in a social sense or an ego sense.

And I'm like, "Oh my God, this is probably what's happened to me!" I read everything I could get my hands on about deep ecology.

Now when I go to the city, I feel naked. I go and I do my little things up there—go to a concert, see my friends, teach. But boy, I can hardly wait to get back here and get my clothes back on. I step out of my car and it's, whew! There's this bigger piece of me here.

And that's the way I felt when I was a kid going into a field of hay. All by myself, I'd climb into the field and go in, and just peer out over the top, and then I'd sit down in the middle. As a kid, you don't have enough boundaries to tell you you are separate. And that's a part of the coming home process that this place has been for me.

Right now, even though I like the solitude, I find myself a little bit hungry to be part of a community. I have friends, but they're far apart. I really am wanting to be with a group of people who are working together. I need the consistency of everyday interaction in a meaningful way, in a purposeful way. I feel that really strongly. I'm hoping that maybe I can gather a few people to work here who will make it feel that way.

I see my purpose in life more clearly now. The way I make my money is Niches, and that money allows me to do my work, which is the healing of this fifty acres, this little piece of the earth.

Tough Guy

Vince Reynolds

I finally got over [the divorce]. I learned to deal with the heartaches. My attitude from Vietnam chipped apart. I learned not to explode at a moment's notice. I learned that I had to focus on what was ahead of me, instead of letting the past consume me. And because I had faced my own problems, I became a lot more understanding of other people's problems.

We learned about Vince Reynolds, a police detective assigned to work with juvenile street gangs, in a newspaper article that announced his official citation for bravery. While cruising the streets to look for gang activity, Vince had seen a burning house and rushed in to pull a woman and her two-year-old son to safety.

Vince, an African-American in his forties who is built and moves like a football player, is wearing a light sports coat, dark tie, tan pants, and polished black dress boots when he meets us at a small restaurant one cold winter afternoon. He looks at us in a quiet, wary manner. It's clear that he's not too sure about what he got himself into when he agreed to give us this interview. We aren't either.

We exchange a few superficial remarks about various topics to make everyone more comfortable. We complain, for example, about the below-zero temperatures. Vince mentions that, just before meeting us, he stopped to buy his hunting dog some snowboots. Our eyes widen. His smile broadens. All of us begin to relax.

Vince grew up as the oldest of six children in a strong, caring family. He has many fond memories of his childhood, particularly of his father, who devoted time to teaching, talking, and playing with his children.

Sold on cultural ideals about the glamour of war, Vince was drafted into the Army when he was eighteen and spent fourteen-and-a-half months in Vietnam during the height of that conflict. His experiences as a soldier and a veteran helped shape him into a hostile, often belligerent man who had difficulties holding a job. His initial interest in law enforcement helped to sustain his ideal of being the Good Warrior. However, a divorce in his thirties inaugurated a period of self-reflection and change, during which he was supported by the camaraderie of his fellow police officers.

Vince became a father for the first time when he was forty years old. This event seems to have allowed him to tap back into the caring family values he experienced growing up. He speaks at length about his love for his son, and he acknowledges that becoming a father has allowed him to develop and express his sensitivity to the people he works with. He has become particularly involved in providing nurturance and adult guidance to young inner-city males.

On the surface, Vince Reynolds looks like a tough guy, maybe even a dangerous guy. Beneath that surface is the man who rocks his son to sleep, and who is capable of saving a woman and her child from a burning house.

I was born January 4, 1947. My father, Robert Edward Reynolds, and my mother, Mary Johnson Reynolds, had six children. I'm the oldest.

My dad, he was a hardworking guy. He only had an eighth-grade education. He was a self-taught individual. He would take me and my brother along and show us how to wire a house, or how to paint, or how to put up dry wall. He taught us how to tear down cars, then fix them up.

My father loved us. He always told us that. He'd hug us. We talked a lot. He gave me a lot of good instruction—sometimes I followed it, and sometimes I didn't. I wish I had followed it more. I would have been better off. He passed away about four years ago. I miss him a lot.

My mom, she was very hardworking, too, and old-fashioned, from Alabama. She instilled in all of us a sense of what to do in life—if you work hard, you'll get what you want. Thirty years ago, she started the child day-care center she just turned over to my sister. My brother and I had to help Mom clean up the day-care center. We didn't get any allowance for it. I think that's how we learned responsibility.

We came up in a very good middle-class home. Mom and Dad were very strict with us. Nobody got into trouble, nobody stepped out of line, because we didn't want to face the wrath of our parents. Mom would go outside and get a switch off a tree in a New York minute and take care of you. We didn't want to deal with Dad either, arouse him, because he could lay the discipline on you if he had to.

When I look back on growing up, I think about *Happy Days*, the television program. I enjoyed growing up. We used to go down to a restaurant that was a cruising spot on Saturday nights. My dad let my brother and me have his old '55 Plymouth, and we kind of souped it up. Today when I drive by that place, I remember all the kids, both black and white. Everybody got along.

I graduated from high school in '65. Played football and wrestled and lettered in both. Ran cross-country, ran track. Played on the baseball team for one year. Sports were just a facet of life, but I wanted to do them all. I think sports are important for men. Because of the competition. "I'm going to prove my prowess." Plus, it looks good to the girls. You want to have a lot of girlfriends, you get on a sports team.

After high school, I went to the university for about a year, but I never really liked it that much. Then I worked for a year. That's when the big "D" hit, the draft. Got drafted into the Army, which I can't say I was really upset about. I was ready. I wanted to see a lot of different places. I wanted to get over there to Vietnam, I wanted to experience what was going on.

I guess the military appealed to me on a couple of bases. My Uncle Harold—we called him "Uncle Doc"—would tell me about his experiences in the Army, show me his uniform. Even as a little kid, it seemed like a life I would enjoy. It wasn't closed in. You had your freedom, the spirit to do what you wanted to do.

I remember, during the '50s and '60s, I loved to watch John Wayne and Audie Murphy movies. It wasn't as much the killing as it was the glory, the sense of adventure. I remember one quote from this Errol Flynn movie. "There's one thing you can't buy, and that's glory." That always stuck with me.

The war was something I wanted to feel. I'd always been a history buff, and I knew this was history. I wanted to be a part of it. Whatever slate was written, I wanted my name to be a part of it.

So anyway, when I got the draft notice in the mail, I was ready. The only thing I regretted was that I had to leave my fiancee behind. I got engaged to Debbie before I went to Vietnam. She waited, and when I came back in 1970, we got married.

I saw a lot of action in Vietnam, saw a lot of people I knew get hurt. But still, it was a big adventure to me. I think I had prepared myself for what I was going to see. I mean, you can never prepare yourself for death or for the kinds of deaths you see in combat. You don't want to see your buddies get hurt; you don't want to see them die. But I think I was as prepared as possible, mentally and physically.

I learned a lot. I learned how to protect myself. I learned how to pay attention. Believing in the Lord didn't hurt. I'm not a religious fanatic, but

I do believe that someone up there takes care of you. I always prayed to God to watch over me and the other guys in my outfit.

Vietnam fascinated me. I loved the people, the culture. One thing about Vietnam…I remember looking up in the sky sometimes. They had the bluest, puffiest clouds I've ever seen, even to this day. That's what I remember most of Vietnam. Those skies. They gave me a real good lease on living at that time.

The villagers were also very interesting to me. Even though there was a war going on, they mostly acted like it was an everyday situation. They went along with their lives like there wasn't any war. They planted their crops, raised their kids. I got to know quite a few of them.

And then my day came to go home. They said, "Go to the supply room and turn in your rifle, your cot, all this stuff." It was time to go. Went to Cam Ranh Bay, got on this big Delta Airlines jet to go home. There was nobody sitting down with you, asking what kind of problems you might have, explaining what you might see when you went back into the world. It was just, "Okay, guys, it's time to leave."

I remember coming through McCord Air Force Base in Washington. It was about 2:30 in the morning. I couldn't believe this. I was totally wiped out. Everybody was getting off the plane, and there were about three hundred people out there with signs protesting. I'm serious. I can laugh about it now, but everybody was pissed. These people were hollering and stuff. At 2:30 in the morning!

I remember seeing my first Afro on the commercial plane coming home. The guy had this big Afro, out to here. You didn't see any Afros in 'Nam. I was totally shocked. I thought, "This boy ain't had no haircut for a few months." The Army didn't tell us what to expect back home, how to deal with things. It took me a few years to adjust.

When I came home, Debbie and I got married. I had this itch. I still wanted to be a part of the Army. And she kept saying no. We came home and settled down in a little apartment in '70.

Life was boring. Didn't like my job. It was boring. I started running around with a pretty rough bunch of guys I had known years ago. I hadn't hung with them when I was in school, because they weren't up to the caliber of the guys who were into sports. I started not coming home at night. I wasn't drinking, because I didn't drink—but I was bad. These guys kind of admired me because I had been to 'Nam and shot people.

During that period, my dad and I were pretty close. But nobody could really tell me anything. Hey, I was a combat veteran. He told me what he thought, but I did what I wanted to do.

My Uncle Harvey, he liked to fish. One day he said, "We're going fishing." I said, "No, I'm going down with these guys and shoot craps." He said, "No, it's a nice day. Let's go out in my boat." So I went. I remember this big ol' catfish. And I had more fun catching that fish. We were laughing and stuff. After that, we went fishing all the time. He'd pick me up, and we'd go fishing. I started migrating away from this group of guys.

But I know I still had an attitude. I'd always had a quick temper, but it was so volatile when I came back from Vietnam that anything would just set me off. I used to carry this little snub-nosed .32 caliber Smith & Wesson every place I went. Every place. Before I joined the service, I had never touched a gun.

I had problems keeping a job. Every place I went in those days, I had a personality conflict. They said I was belligerent, uncooperative.

Then I graduated with an associate's degree in business administration. Me and Debbie bought a house on the G.I. Bill. Everything started looking real good. Debbie encouraged me a lot.

When I was with the Second Armored Division, I had worked as an M.P. sometimes on a replacement basis. I enjoyed that work, so I went down to the city police department, the first time in June 1970. I took my application up to the sergeant. He looked at me and said, "You a Vietnam veteran?" I said, "Yes, sir."

He tore up my application in four pieces and said, "Well, we're not taking any black Vietnam veterans right now." Just like you and me sitting here, talking. He says, "We find them too mentally unstable for the job." I just got up and walked out of the room. That hurt me, hurt me really bad.

Before I got on the force in '76, I had tried three other times. Every time it was something else they didn't like. Like one time they said my vision couldn't be corrected to 20/20, which was a lie.

When I finally got accepted on the force, I worked on patrol for a couple of years. Then I got into the burglary squad, part of the detective bureau. Somebody saw I did a good job and asked me if I wanted to come and work in the organized-crime bureau—the elite bureau. I got transferred down there in May of '84. That's where I first started working drugs and gangs. From 1984 until now, I've been in the organized-crime intelligence bureau.

When I first got in, I worked undercover. I played dope man out there on the streets. I got to know a lot of dope dealers. A guy can't work like that too long because, after a while, you start taking on the same mannerisms. You start acting like a dope dealer, even around your family. But still, it was exciting living on the edge.

But the job caused problems in communications between me and Debbie. As a cop, you devote a lot more time to the people you're working with than you do to your family, so Debbie and I grew apart. I guess it was a combination of stuff, stuff I had carried over from Vietnam, too. It just snowballed for both of us. She was a good woman, but we got divorced in 1984.

Debbie and I were so materialistic and career-oriented when we were young. We wanted to get all this stuff as we got better pay. If we had had children, I think we might have been more solid. But we didn't have any. There was nothing there to make us deal with our problems. There was no reason to stay. We were married almost seventeen years.

Debbie wanted the house. Said she wouldn't ask for any of my police pension fund. I thought, "Hell, I can always buy another house." But I had put my emotions into that house. It was a house I had bought when I came back from Vietnam.

There's something about working and planning and doing stuff, and then having to leave it. The divorce and leaving that house dug at me. I had to talk to a therapist in order to get through it. I recognized I had to do something. The feeling reminded me of when I came back from Vietnam, all the pressures. The therapist said, "You have to put yourself into something and get your mind off it." So I did.

I got myself involved in a special street-crime unit, and I worked that stuff seven days a week for a while. The guys on my unit, they really helped me. I talked to them about the divorce and how hard it had been to leave the house. The camaraderie was just like in 'Nam. We were like brothers.

I finally got over it. I learned to deal with the heartaches. My attitude from Vietnam chipped apart. I learned not to explode at a moment's notice. I learned that I had to focus on what was ahead of me, instead of letting the past consume me. And because I had faced my own problems, I became a lot more understanding of other people's problems.

I had been divorced just over a year when I got married again. One of the things that has helped both of us is having children. My wife had a son from a previous marriage, and we had another son together. And we both adore him. I'm forty-six. It was a real turning point to have a child when I was forty.

I'm glad I have children at this point. I think I make a better father now than I would have when I was younger. I know I'm more nurturing. I used to sit and rock and hold Bobby when he was a little baby, listen to him coo. I never thought a guy could do that, especially a guy who hunts and fishes and stuff like that. I think that the caring I got from my mother and father has come back to me so that I can give it to my son.

Bobby is six years old now. I love him, I really do. We go to the movies all the time. We go fishing. He wants to tag along with me all the time. We play and wrestle together. I spend as much time as I can with him. Like today, I went to the school and talked to his class. Even now, he cuddles with me in my lounge chair and goes to sleep. That's the best feeling in the world. My stepson, Jason, he's thirteen years old. He's a good kid. We get along. I don't try to be his father, but I try to be a role model to him. I show him love. I want him to know I'll take care of him, try to help him if he needs it. We sit and talk. I don't come across heavyhanded. I expect him to carry out his responsibilities at home, but I do understand that kids forget sometimes.

I have come to see that giving more to my kids and doing less for myself can be enjoyable. I've learned how to balance things with both boys—not to be overbearing and not to be weak. I think I'm doing a pretty good job.

I guess my experiences with my own son have increased my interest in working with kids out on the street. Some of those boys have no fathers, no one they can talk to. I like to sit and talk with them and let them talk to me. I find they really appreciate that. They open up.

I try, especially with young black males, to show them some caring and teach them some self-respect. I want them to have the attitude that, whatever job you have, you should be the best at that job. That's what my father always taught me.

I've taken some of the younger boys fishing with me. Because they've never been fishing. Some of them have never been out of their six-block neighborhood. They've never seen wildlife. They may never get to do it again, but—at least one time in their life—they had somebody who cared enough to take them fishing. It may make a difference.

I think that's what a lot of these kids need, to get out of that environment. They need to see something beyond the drug dealers and prostitutes in their neighborhood. They need to get out in the fresh air where there aren't gunshots and people arguing.

When I was young, I was always very quick to act, and this got me into trouble. I didn't take my time and look the situation over. I think that's what happened with my first marriage. I was too quick to act. Over the years, I have learned to investigate more, find out more, look past the first thing I see. I'm also a lot more self-reflective.

Since January, I've been to ten kids' funerals, kids between fourteen and seventeen years old. So this is what I tell the kids out there on the street who are tempted to join up with a gang, "Take your time making your choice, because it's going to be the most important choice in your life. The gang road may look real good, studded with gold and dollar bills, but it's a very short road really. Or you can take the long road. It's studded with a lot of barriers, but if you stay on this road, you can fulfill your dreams."

It is definitely important to me to make a difference with these kids. Maybe it's my calling. In any case, I do enjoy it.

Letting the Warts Show

Nick Reiser

If you're a five-year-old, everything that happens to you is monumental. But if you've lived fifty years, you've done a lot of monumental living. If something sad happens, it's still sad, but it's buffered by other events in life that say, "Things go on." There's enough to draw upon by now in my life to allow me to put things in perspective. I'm comfortable with this. It's a feeling of settledness.

A mutual friend introduced us to Nick Reiser, a mental health counselor, at a Christmas party. In the course of conversation, we mentioned that we were working on a book about midlife men. Nick was very enthusiastic and strongly encouraged us to see it through. The following summer, we drove to Marietta, Georgia, to run some of our ideas by him and to interview him as a subject for the book.

Nick is a tall, solidly built man. His black hair is thinning on top, his square jaw softened by a bushy mustache. He wears a red plaid sports shirt with the sleeves rolled up on his forearms, and khaki slacks. He has a pleasant, reassuring smile and a low, hoarse-sounding voice.

Nick is a self-reflective man who has traced the process of his life growth from the influences of family, career, and marriage. He talks about how he has changed from being a detached, intensely intellectual person in his young adulthood to a man who now shares himself emotionally with others.

He explains how, since entering midlife, he has learned the values of humor, flexibility, and pleasing himself as well as other people. Nick believes these life changes have come naturally from within, through keeping in touch with what makes him feel good about himself professionally as well as personally, and by taking thoughtful risks to develop this identity.

A twenty-seven-year career path had gradually led Nick into administration. A couple of years ago, however, he made the move back to direct counseling with clients, which he finds more satisfying, especially because he feels that his matured sense of self allows him to be more effective as a counselor.

Nick remarried for the third time a year ago after a careful, gradual development of commitment. To this marriage he also brings a matured sense of how to deal with another person's differences, how to be supportive, and how to recognize support.

At fifty, Nick happily acknowledges the sense of wholeness and rightness he has about himself, his career, and his marriage.

I'm from Milwaukee originally. Hungarian and German heritage. Immigrant background. My early models were my grandfather and, to a lesser degree, my father.

In terms of growing up, I remember some rather set patterns in the family. For example, eating. The children—*die kinder*—got served first, then the men, then the women. Eating was very respectable in my family. If the children ate a lot, if the adults ate a lot, that was wonderful. Eating and preparing food were ways of showing love and respect and giving attention.

My grandmother was also an important model for me. We lived with my grandparents for a while, and my grandmother was always taking care of me. She would have me clean the sink, which I liked to do. She would reward me for being quiet. She would say, "Oh, Nick is such a good boy. So quiet. You would hardly notice he was here." I think the shy part of me comes from that idea that you're good if you're quiet. You're quiet, and you get a reward. Of course, as an adult, you don't get much reward if you're quiet.

I played some baseball and went swimming as a kid. Read comic books. I didn't realize until maybe the seventh grade that I was kind of a nerd. I didn't have that many friends. Just kind of went about my business. I remember I wore a sailor hat that I bent down like Gilligan when I was in junior high. I guess other people thought I was an odd kid.

In high school, I was a lifeguard at the pool. I was a swimmer. I played football in junior high and high school. Basketball in junior high and high. Ran some track. Wasn't sexually active, just necking. Never went steady. "How'd you make out? Did you get any?" Even then, I thought such phrases were offensive. I didn't get into the locker-room stuff.

My best friend in high school had an older brother who is still a friend to this day. About ten years my senior, he was a psychologist. Looking back on it now, I can see how he was saying some of the same things that my parents were saying, but it seemed different coming from him. Coming from him, it was significant and believable.

He would be complimentary or give advice, say things like, "You ought to try this." I would attend to that, listen to him because he was so smart.

He was a mentor in terms of my professional ambitions. I remember he had a habit of clicking his tongue against his cheek. I started doing it, too.

The first and the second half of my college years were totally different. The first half I didn't do very well. I remember the dean recommended speed reading, which was a big thing in those days because Kennedy had gone to Evelyn Wood. After that, I tested real high in terms of speed and comprehension. I hadn't read much up until that point. I started buying tons of books. And I read everything.

After I graduated with a degree in psychology in the late '60s, I went to work at a prison as a correctional counselor. That was my first introduction to reality. It was a good professional experience. Met some interesting people, a black man who was my introduction to the civil rights movement. In high school, I had often walked home with black peers who lived in a neighborhood next to the one my parents lived in. I didn't understand how people could hate other people.

My next job was in a community center. I got a lot of experience there working with black and white kids. I got beat up once trying to stop a fight between two kids. It was a volatile time. It was a rich time, though, learning about relationships between the races.

Two-and-a-half years after I graduated, I went on to grad school. I didn't particularly try to get out of being drafted to Vietnam—it just kind of happened with school and then working in the prison. There was a part of me that debated whether to sign up, because I figured I was going to get drafted. But I kept getting occupational deferments.

I met my first wife, Mary, in grad school. Maybe six months after grad school, we got married. Had two kids. I got more into administrative work and away from service with clients.

Mary and I were married about eight years. We were both of us inexperienced. Actually, she was my first serious relationship. It takes a long time, generally, for me to make up my mind and commit. But once I've committed, I get tunnel vision.

We were divorced about '76. We responded to each other differently. I was laid back, cool. She wanted somebody to fight back, so when I didn't fight back, that meant, for her, rejection. I didn't see that at the time.

Our family backgrounds clashed, too. She was raised with all sisters. Her father was an alcoholic, and her acquaintance with men was filtered through her sisters and mother. I was raised in a culturally male-oriented family. The women served the men. Quite a difference. But there were no issues about the kids for either of us.

Looking back on it, it was a bitter divorce. But as with all experiences, over time I'm sure it served a purpose. I hardly think about it anymore.

Being divorced was such an abrupt change for me. For months, I was very active socially and had to go out and be with people all the time. I was always in some self-improvement program. One night, it was a Friday or Saturday, I got in the car. I remember it was cold, wintertime. And I couldn't figure out where I was going. I had started the engine even, but I couldn't figure out where I was going.

I sat there and I sat there. And then I got out of the car, and I went back inside. At that moment, there was a kind of revelation, a revelation that I could be okay as is, physically and psychologically. I didn't have to be going someplace, or be with somebody, to be okay.

From then on, I started handling my life differently. I started relaxing about being divorced, about being alone. Sometimes I went out, and sometimes I didn't. My life flowed better.

I got married a second time, to Susan, five years after my divorce. That marriage lasted about eighteen months. I don't regret it. I don't think I would have married Susan if—I don't mean this as self-flattery—she hadn't pursued me. Because I wasn't particularly interested in getting married again.

She had an affair with another man, and the marriage ended. My divorce with Susan was somewhat painful, but it wasn't as bad as when my first marriage ended. That's how Susan's first marriage had ended, with an affair. I think it was just kind of in her nature. After the divorce, I moved to Kentucky to work for about three years with disturbed kids in a juvenile center.

My career has never been planned very well. It just kind of happened. Somebody knew about me, called me, and I had a job. I moved all over the place, from a family service agency, to a prison, to an epilepsy center, to a halfway house for juveniles, lots of stuff with kids, all kinds of counseling. That's really been the strength of my career, that versatility.

The traditional thing in my profession is that you go from direct service, where you don't earn much, to management positions higher up in the organization. The further removed you are from the people, the more money you make.

In the last couple of years, I've gone back to where my career started—to direct counseling. Being detached from people conflicted with the direction I wanted to go, both personally and professionally. I took a twenty-five percent cut in pay to go back to client work, but it was where I wanted to go.

I'm in a different place with my career now. When I first started out in counseling, clients looked at me as professionally objective and detached. I was pretty introspective, intellectual. I had read the books, but I didn't have much life experience to go on. People would talk about their marriage, their kids, their intimate problems, and I was always up in my head, not in my heart, when I tried to help them.

Now I've rounded the corner by living my life, paying my dues. I've done more than just read about life. I've gone through marriage, divorce, kids. These things are just a part of life growth, but they've also given me something to share with clients. I feel more emotionally capable. A parent comes in to talk about his child now, I can really empathize. I've been there.

I'm much more direct and interactive because I feel comfortable with what I'm doing. When I was younger and starting out, I wouldn't have said to a client, "Come on, you know better than that." Now I'll do that. "Come on." I'll confront in a gentle way. I'll nudge.

I'm also more flexible about being emotional with my clients. I'm much more self-revealing. I try to draw parallels with clients from my own life without sounding too hokey.

For example, I have this client, very cynical, who's always looking for a straw man, an excuse for not doing something with his life. I told him about when I used to be a lifeguard, how I'd sit there watching the kids whose mothers kept saying, "Come on, get in now." And these kids looked miserable. They weren't having fun at all. Then there were these other kids who just kind of—cowabunga!—jumped in. They'd be having a ball. They weren't worrying about it or contemplating it—they were just doing it.

I wouldn't have drawn on my own experiences like that when I was young, making them fit into some appropriate context. Now I use this technique. I tell stories about my family, my friends, maybe even my cats. And it works.

I'm fifty years old now. My life is more whole than it's ever been. I have a perspective on life. I recently got together with two old friends, one a recently retired psychologist. We were talking, and one of the things we all three almost simultaneously got into was what it's like being older. The difference is that we've got continuity and experience to draw upon.

If you're a five-year-old, everything that happens to you is monumental. But if you've lived fifty years, you've done a lot of monumental living. If something sad happens, it's still sad, but it's buffered by other events in life that say, "Things go on." There's enough to draw upon by now in my life to allow me to put things in perspective. I'm comfortable with this. It's a feeling of settledness.

I've been married now again for about a year. A friend introduced us. We first got together over some beers. Apparently, I presented my resume while we were talking. I guess I was a bore.

The first or second date, we went to the movies and saw *Moonstruck*, which was apparently the wrong movie. I guess I wore some kind of nerdy clothes, too, white pants or something you don't wear anymore—something like my sailor hat.

She was feeling uncomfortable, and I was feeling uncomfortable because she was uncomfortable. When we got back to her house, she offered me a beer, and our joke now is that I felt like I should have said to her, "Is this beer for the road?" And she did want me to go, apparently.

Then we started dating more regularly. I remember she had sexual concerns, and she didn't know quite how to deal with them in spite of the experience she's had as a counselor of socially transmitted diseases. She asked me for a sexual history before we went to bed for the first time. Was I screwing around with other women? Was I clean?

About a year after we started dating, I moved in with her. Then we bought a house together. It was gradual commitment. I think for Rita it was important to get married. As I said to her, it doesn't mean any more of a commitment for me. I became committed to her when I moved in with her.

Our marriage at this age involves different tasks than my first marriage, when we had to raise children and deal with the diaper pail. We find other ways of adjusting to the other person's quirks than we did when we were younger.

From a relationship standpoint, I'm much less likely to brood and be introspective. And I'm more flexible. When we have a big fight, we might say, "I know you're mad at me, and I'm mad at you. What I did was shitty, and what you did was shitty. We might need some time to lick our wounds, but then let's get on with it." It's a mellowing out, I guess. You realize things aren't a big deal, and you put them in better perspective. You let your warts show.

Sex is different, too. It's more enjoyable, yet qualitatively different. I don't feel a sense of horniness all the time, running around with an erection. I'm not saying take it or leave it. I definitely don't want to leave it. But it's much more relaxed. Sex is just one facet of who I am. I see snuggling as much more important than the hot-and-heavy stuff.

What's important to me now is my marriage and my kids. The kids are adults now. They've been such a central part of my life all these years, regardless of what else was going on. Visits were very regular, and we did a lot of things together as they were growing up.

In midlife, as I look back on how they've become adults, I'm very pleased. I'm also kind of humbled by them. As a young parent, I was confident that you could shape your children. I found out I was wrong. You plant a seed, and it continues to grow. You do shape them, but the influence is a lot less than you think. They make their own decisions. They figure out what works best for them.

Sometimes I have difficulty relating to my kids as adults. I admit I'm still a bit awkward there. Not that I want to treat them as kids, but having known them as kids, sometimes it's hard to realize that I can't tell them to brush their teeth anymore. Rita, my wife, has been a model for me in dealing with my kids as adults. I'm learning from how she talks to the kids, and from how they talk to her.

And I'm starting to learn to please myself. I'm letting loose. When I was younger—teens, early twenties, up to the first divorce—I was much more serious. After that divorce, I decided I wanted to develop my sense of humor. It was a way for me to socialize comfortably. I literally practiced getting myself able to say oneliners, making up jokes and puns.

I continue to use humor to lighten myself up. It helps me to laugh at myself, and to make other people laugh and feel comfortable. I find I'm better able to pace myself with humor. I don't get burned out anymore by work demands. I kind of pace myself like an old hound does, just walking along. I'll get there when I get there.

I'm much more able to give, too, and that's important to me. Before, in my younger years, I gave because I felt that I ought to give. Like the mother serving the kids first because she *should* do it. That was a part of me for a long time.

I've rejected that. Now I do things because I want to. Like walking with my wife. I used to think I should do it because I know it's important to her and I know it's good for my own health. What's different is now I want to do it. I don't say to myself, "I'll do it so she'll shut up about it." And I don't say, "What a wonderful person I am for doing it," the martyr attitude. It's neither of those. I want to do it, and I want to do it with her.

That's important because it allows me to extend myself in a more honest way, rather than because of the voices of my parents, and my parents' parents, playing on tapes in my brain.

I'm not sure I can be precise about how these changes started. They've just sort of evolved over the years as part of a development process. I can best explain the changes with an analogy, I guess—tying shoes.

I get up in the morning and tie my shoes, and I don't even think about it. But when I was learning, I was all thumbs, awkward and confused. I had to think about which lace went where. I think this learning mode applies to other things throughout life. The ability to use humor or to be more emotionally involved—it was very uncomfortable at first. But I've worked at it, and I've refined it more and more. Now it's become automatic. And it's that flow, that ease that allows me to enjoy what it is I'm doing. It also gives me a sense of what's important.

Another part of midlife for me has been that I see myself as less unique, less isolated. There's a photograph of my second- or third-grade class, and if you look at it, you can see a physical distance between me and the rest of the group, a noticeable gap. And I think that's the way I've felt in my life as a shy, intellectual person. In my twenties and thirties, that was still very much a part of me and the way that I treated clients. I kept my distance. The administrative work allowed me to do that, too.

As a result of seeing and relating to what other people have experienced over the years, I've come to realize I'm not this totally unique person I thought I was when I was younger. And that's nice. It makes me feel more like a part of humanity.

The World's Greatest Second Banana

Don Grayson

> By changing courses midstream, some very positive things
> have happened to me. I no longer desire the wealth, the
> stuff. There are some things I want. Certainly not the
> Mercedes and the Jaguar anymore. I'm perfectly happy
> today with a fishing pole and a pickup truck. That's impor-
> tant to me today.

*Don Grayson, a fifty-year-old tobacco store owner, is a man so completely
at ease with himself that he makes others feel at ease as well. He is a down-
home, Kentucky kind of guy. Hospitable. Gentlemanly. But the positive and
extroverted persona he presents to the world is only part of who he is. He is
also a reflective man who, as he approached midlife, felt compelled to ask
himself important questions.*

*His former career as a computer engineer had beckoned him up the
corporate ladder with its accompanying lifestyle trappings. Upward mobility
and material success were the standards for manhood in corporate life. But
the pleasures of the "good life" wore thin and were replaced, in Don's thirties,
by vague feelings of dissatisfaction.*

*His awakening at midlife was precipitated by an unexpected, unwanted
divorce. The unconscious anger he felt at that rejection spawned a destruc-
tive pattern of rejecting women. Reflection on this behavior was the first step
toward a radical change of values. His subsequent introduction to Taoism,
with its emphasis on non-striving, helped him to make sense of his discontent
and led to a new life philosophy, as well as a new career path.*

*Don is now more aware of his feelings than he was as a younger man.
The deaths of two people who were close to him, one of whom was his father,
have affected him profoundly. These encounters with death have tapped his
vulnerability and taught him to share his grief with others. Facing the
inevitability of death has also affirmed and deepened his new resolve to
"experience life" rather than try to control it.*

*The interview takes place in the living room of the home Don shares
with his current wife and lifelong friend, Patti. The many cultural and
religious artifacts that decorate the room reflect their shared interest in
Eastern religions.*

Displayed among the reminders of ancient cultures are three clay pots Don has handcrafted. They seem symbolic of the Taoist philosophy he now embraces. The designs are strong, the edges worked smooth. Don has made use of simple lines and subtle glazes. These earthy, stone-like vessels are fine pieces, and it is hard to believe these are his first attempts at pottery making.

Finding out who we are—discovering our "right" place in life—often serves to free up our creative expression so that what is created is more like who we really are. Don's willingness to work through the uncomfortable feelings that emerged as he approached midlife brought him new images of male strength to replace the ones he had embraced as a young man.

I was an only child. I was raised in a small town in eastern Kentucky, one of those towns where everybody knows everybody. It was impossible for me to get away with anything because everybody knew me.

I had a storybook boyhood, really. The neighborhood we lived in was filled with children my age. Patti, my wife, grew up in the neighborhood. We were surrounded by woods. We played there, we hiked there—we'd spend all day in those woods. And there were caves. We told ghost stories about the caves in those woods, and they got passed on to the younger kids.

I think I had an idyllic childhood. I really do. My father taught me to shoot. We went hunting and fishing together, all those things you nowadays only read about men and their fathers doing. It was just that kind of experience.

I guess one of the roughest times in my life was when I was starting out in college. I was having a lot of difficulty finding out who I was. It was my first time in a situation where I was really handling myself. I was out there on my own, and I had some identity problems.

In high school, I had always been in the "in" group, the clique. I was fairly popular. When you get away to college and start meeting other people who are more intelligent than you and better looking than you, suddenly you feel the competition. So I really didn't do well early on in college, although at some point I adjusted.

I graduated with an associate degree in electrical engineering. This whole thing with electronics just kind of materialized. You know, if you wanted a career with a future in those days, you got into electronics.

This was when the Russians were putting up Sputnik and the space program was getting started, the early '60s. John Kennedy had just been elected, and he had plans to put a man on the moon. The future was wide open. Computers were just coming on strong. I decided that maybe electronics was the way to go. I had started out in accounting because my father had been an accountant. So this was my first real attempt to break free, to be my own person.

I had met and fallen in love with my first wife, Marianne, while I was in my final year of school. After graduation, I went to work for a major computer corporation and bought a little mobile home. At the time, it was all I could afford.

I went on active duty with the National Guard for nine months, about four months after we got married. I had a lot of friends who were going off to Vietnam at that time, and some were not coming back. Vietnam was something I wanted to avoid. I was very much opposed to the war.

In fact, I sat down one time and had a talk with my father about it. My father was a veteran of World War II. I mean, he was kind of a flag-waver, very patriotic. I told him, "If I get a draft notice, I may just go to Canada. It's either Canada or jail because, in good conscience, I just can't fight the war in Vietnam." I was surprised when he agreed with me. He said he would support me one hundred percent.

At that time in my life I was into this control thing, into "acting upon life," manipulating so I could achieve the things I wanted to achieve. Because that was what you *did*. If you went to any of the motivational programs at that time, that's what they were all about—you know, taking life and running with it.

I was into that. I really was. And my company encouraged it. I would watch for opportunities to move into positions that would give me a higher profile. And I got promotions. I got pay raises.

Marianne and I bought a beautiful townhouse. We furnished it beautifully. It was right out of a magazine. We were really into that sort of thing. We had a Mercedes Benz and a Jaguar XKE. It was very pleasant. I mean, on the weekend, you go out and you jump in your Jag and go out for a night on the town.

But somewhere in my early thirties, the bubble started to burst. Something wasn't right. We had all of this stuff, but there was something important we didn't have, and we didn't know what it was.

The marriage started to falter. We started having problems—minor at first, then escalating. Marianne started having longer and deeper depressions.

She'd always been bothered by depressions, but they were usually just for a week or so, or maybe a few days.

Then she started staying in these depressions for two or three months at a time. Just totally withdrawn. She had no interest in communicating with me. And there was nothing I could do to help her out of it. It was extremely frustrating.

At that point in my life, I didn't have enough sense to go out and find out something about depression. I think today if the same thing happened, I would try to find out more about it—read about it or talk to somebody who might be able to help.

One Sunday afternoon as Marianne, who was a nurse, was leaving to work the evening shift, I could tell there was something wrong. And I just asked her, in a concerned way, what it was. She turned to me and said, "I want a divorce. I don't want to be married anymore."

I almost fell down the stairs. I mean, it just knocked the props out from under me. It's something I had never considered. On the one hand, you have this nagging feeling that something is wrong, but really, it's not that bad. You think the marriage can be fixed, or it'll come back, or whatever.

I couldn't get her to talk about it. She just didn't want to be married anymore, and that's all she could say. It was just like—blam!—like being broadsided, you know?

I was bewildered. I was shocked. I was blaming myself because I thought I had done something. I was totally distraught. And the first thing I thought of was that I really needed to talk to Patti.

Patti and I had grown up together and had always confided in each other. I mean, we talked about everything. I've never been as close to anybody in my life as I have been to her. I always felt comfortable asking her advice, just bouncing things off her.

We arranged times to talk. Patti encouraged me and tried to help me think through things that might get the relationship back on track. Because, at that time, my intent was to keep this marriage going. Patti could see that was what I wanted, all the while cautioning me that it might not work out.

Basically, that was the beginning of our life together—even though neither of us knew it at the time. We didn't have the least inkling we would end up together.

But Marianne and I did end up in divorce, and I started my four years of bachelorhood—which I'm glad happened in 1977, not in the '80s, because I sowed a lot of wild oats. I did it partly from anger. I was out for the pleasure in life. The partying. The women. Whatever. I was in a position where I had money and could do pretty much what I wanted to do. And I could do it in style.

I had a pretty wild life. I left some baggage behind. I know I did. I hate to admit it, but I was down on women, and I hurt some of them. I shouldn't have directed my anger at the entire gender, but I did.

I was kind of a silver-tongued devil. I talked a good talk, but it wasn't what I was really feeling. It was a means to an end. I didn't realize what was going on at the time. I would just lose interest. There were three women in about a three-year period who built up some hopes about a commitment.

For me, the conquest had become more important than the relationship. Once I achieved what I wanted, a sexual outcome, the relationship began to fall off.

I really didn't start putting it together until after it had happened a third time and I started losing interest again. Then it was like, "Whoa, what's going on here? What are you doing?"

Finally, I realized that the hard part of the divorce had been the feeling of rejection, of someone saying, "I don't want you anymore. I don't love you. There's nothing that you have that I want anymore." I had never experienced that before. And this was someone who at one time *had* thought that I was a valuable individual. All of a sudden, I wasn't anymore. And that really cut to the core.

Later, I called some women back and made some apologies. I tried to at least let them know that I realized what I had done. That I was not proud of it.

I don't understand this completely, but when I realized that I really was in love with Patti, the anger suddenly left. I recognized what I had been doing, what I had been feeling.

I was about thirty-seven when I started feeling a lot of dissatisfaction. I didn't know where these negative feelings were coming from or what they were, although I had always had a feeling that something was not quite right about this "acting upon life." I was making life go the way I wanted it to go, but there was something down deep inside, something I pushed just as far down as I could, that kept saying, "Wait a minute. You may be missing something here. You're forcing life, instead of experiencing life."

When Patti and I began seeing each other, I took a weekend college course she was teaching—a comparative religion course. That was my real breakthrough. That's when I realized who I was, what I was, what my life was about.

When I heard about Taoism in Patti's course, suddenly I had a name for the dissatisfaction I was feeling. I had an almost immediate recognition that Taoism was the only thing that would really work.

The Taoist philosophy is about moving, flowing with life instead of acting upon it. Like coming to a rock in the middle of a stream. Instead of beating against that rock to get around it, you become like water, flowing around it. Taoism is key to me. Having the full experience of life. Watching. Observing. Learning.

I started looking really hard at everything I was doing in my life. My job, my friends, my associations, my dating. Everything. Just looking at it and seeing where I was doing just the opposite of what I felt was right because, somewhere along the line in one of these motivational programs I had taken years earlier, someone had said you have to get ahead.

I suddenly thought, "What does 'get ahead' mean?" I had had everything. I had had the beautiful townhouse. I had had the big cars, the nice clothes. I had had all the money. And all of a sudden, because my wife decided to leave the marriage, it was all gone.

So here I'd been, acting upon life. Accumulating. And what did it bring me in the end? The loss of everything. It brought me misery, so to speak. Because not only had I not wanted the marriage to end, I had wanted all this accumulating to go on, too.

Once I started thinking about it, I saw that getting ahead wasn't really important. There is a biblical passage that goes, "What does it gain a man if he gains the whole world and loses his soul?" I felt like that was what had been happening. I was gaining stuff and losing my self.

About the time I was sorting all this out, I was becoming dissatisfied with the company I worked for. Things were going on, things that I had practiced myself—like, anything that got in the way of making money, even if it was the right thing to do, you didn't do it because the most important thing was the "bottom line."

That way of thinking really started to bother me. The accumulation, the high profile, the achievement left me cold, empty. I wanted to make a complete and total change in my life. I guess this was my midlife crisis.

I had to change my life. So I left the company in 1981. That was the date of my rebirth.

At that time, Patti and I lived in different cities, and I would go to see her on the weekends. Our birthdays are only a couple of weeks apart, so some friends gave us a fortieth birthday party. I realized then, for the first time, that my feelings for her were more than just the feelings you have for a sister or a close friend. I really loved her, in a romantic way. It was a complete and total love.

She was still married, and, of course, we didn't act upon our feelings. But then—fortunately or unfortunately, depending on how you look at it— her relationship ended, too. When that happened, ours became a real romantic relationship.

I moved to where Patti lived, and eventually we got married. Up to this point in my life, this marriage is definitely the best thing that's ever happened to me. Suddenly, not only do I have a best friend, she's my wife, too. That's the best of all possible worlds right there. You have everything you need when your best friend is your wife, or your husband. There's not much more you can ask for.

Patti has opened me up in so many ways, from the closed-down, don't-show-anything executive type I was to who I am today. We've been good for each other. And even though we're married—and a lot of times marriage inhibits communication—we've still been able to maintain the communication we've had since we were six years old. The ability to talk about anything.

We talk about problems we have in the relationship, problems with other family members, world situations—we talk about anything and everything. We probably spend an hour out of every day just talking to each other. I think that's probably pretty unusual.

And we accept each other, too, for who and what we are. Because we've watched each other grow up, we know each other's background, and we know why we are what we are.

Today I am the world's greatest second banana. I no longer like a high-profile position. I like the Ed McMahon position. It's also the way my marriage goes. Patti is the high-profile one in the marriage, the one with the causes and the missions, which I support. I'm a good support guy.

When we were first married, I decided I would go back to college. The course I took from Patti had sparked my interest in learning new things.

So I began taking some more courses. I thought about going into marketing or something. But the more I thought about it, the more I realized I was getting back into the same old mode where you're trying to influence the whole world, trying to get them to buy your product.

Ever since I was seventeen years old, I have been interested in pipes and smoking and that sort of thing. I decided to follow that interest, and I sought a job in a little shop that sold pipes and cigars and smoking implements of all kinds. I just walked into the shop cold—I didn't call or anything. Lo and behold, the guy who owned the shop was in need of a full-time employee.

I worked there for a while, then started my own business. When that didn't work out, I went to work for another tobacco store. Pete, the owner, was a young man who eventually came down with cancer. When he got sick, I ran the business so as to allow him to do his best to fight the disease, to be with his family and not worry about the business. Pete was not only my employer, he was my friend. So I was suffering with him through his disease and his death.

Getting through that two-year period of Pete's illness was tough for me. Getting through the funeral was tough for me. I'm the kind of guy who, when I grieve, I grieve. I just wash my laundry right in public. There would be times at the store—and this happened after my dad died, too—I would be talking to somebody, and you can't help it, but the grief overcomes you. The tears well up. Men aren't supposed to cry, but it happens.

Pete and I were a super team, just a super team. I really miss those days. Now I run the business in partnership with his wife, and I still love what I'm doing.

This business is like a little "Cheers." A lot of people just hang around all the time. It's a popular place. People like to sit and have a smoke, or drink a little coffee. So I've made a lot of friends. And I've learned to grieve openly even though that's a tough thing to do for a male. It really is.

I guess it's a macho thing. I can't get around it. There is this macho thing about crying and grieving openly. But I was so close to Pete. And he died so young. I still miss him.

I've only had a few close friends like that in my life, friends I've felt comfortable with and can talk about anything with. I think it's really tough for men to tell intimate things to other men. You're supposed to be strong. You're supposed to be self-sufficient. You're the provider, the breadwinner, the hunter. You can't let yourself be vulnerable.

There's a sizing up, a competitiveness among men, all the time. And there's an aspect of nature in all this. Let's say you've got a herd of deer, and you've got the one buck trying to keep all these does together. And around the perimeter, there's all these other younger bucks, all the time. They're waiting. Just one sign of weakness, and bam! You've lost your horns.

I think that same thing is present with men. Back here in this primal brain, there's still a lot of stuff stashed away that's pure survival. You still feel that there may be a potential predator out there. Danger. Somebody moving in on your territory. Whatever that may be. It may not be your wife or your family. It may be your job. It may be some other aspect of your life.

In the last few years, I've measured my life in inches and not in miles. It's not important to me to save the world, but if I can help one person get through today, that's fine. I may never see that person again, but if I smile when they need a smile or offer an encouraging word when they need it, that's what's important. I ask what I can do right now.

It's exciting to me to just sit back and watch things develop. I believe, if we live this way, that life will take its natural course. For instance, just being there for Pete, who needed me very much. Had I really "acted upon" my life and decided, "By golly, I want the big job"—president of the company—I may have missed that opportunity completely.

By changing courses midstream, some very positive things have happened to me. I no longer desire the wealth, the *stuff.* There are some things I want, but certainly not the Mercedes and the Jaguar anymore. I'm perfectly happy today with a fishing pole and a pickup truck. That's important to me today.

I've always loved nature and the outdoors. Recently Patti and I bought a piece of property we fell in love with down in the hills, about an hour from here. It's quite a bit like the woods back in Kentucky. It's very hilly, very rocky, a lot of cliffs and rock outcroppings.

We've put in a tremendous amount of work cutting a road back into the property and cutting trees. We knew it was going to be tough when we started, but we loved the property. We can go down and just spend all afternoon napping in the warm sunshine, listening to the wind blow through the trees, watching the wildlife.

It's very peaceful, very quiet. I can just hike around with my walking stick and a canteen on my hip and spend the whole day there. It's someplace where I can go and really renew. I can feel the tension and the stress from work dissolve while I'm there.

And there are these pots I make. I've never thought of myself as a creative individual, but I've always been kind of enthralled by ceramic pots. I really appreciate them. When Patti and I would go to the art fairs, I would always be drawn to where the pottery was. She suggested I take a pottery class.

So I decided, "Yeah, I'll do that." It's not something I had been longing for years to do. It's just something that was suggested, and I decided, "Yeah, that sounds neat." I love to make coil pots and slab pots. The ones I've made just happened, basically. Doing it, making these forms, and *seeing* it happen is very gratifying. It really is. It's very therapeutic. I really feel that now, after forty-nine years, my life is on course, that things are happening the way they should.

My father's death a few months ago has also brought some real changes in my life. His death has put me one step closer to my own mortality. That can be horrifying or enlightening, depending on how you handle it. There is nothing between me and the great nothingness now. My mother is still alive, that's true, but I sort of patterned myself after my father. When I looked ahead of me, I saw my father. And now that slot is empty. I've just moved up a slot.

There's been a quickening of the senses, an experiential thing that's hard to describe. Life has become a little sweeter. Life can be more exciting, sometimes, when you're on the edge. Because I am out on the edge of the envelope now, from the standpoint of nothing standing between me and death. The door is wide open. It's not something I fear or something that creeps into my mind every day. It's just something that's there.

Artist and Elder

Richard Suazo

I welcome growing old because of how my life has changed. Turning forty is a coming of age for me because I have only bloomed in the last six years. I don't know where I was from the time I was born until six years ago. But everything that's happened to me since has been towards growth. I've never talked about this with anybody. I keep my seeking very, very private. I go up on a mountain, and I cry if I have to. I don't hide anything from myself. And because of that, my life is just going to be more growth.

We arrive at Taos Pueblo in New Mexico on a hot June afternoon, the day of the Corn Dance. Although the dance is scheduled for one o'clock, we are told the ceremony will actually begin only when the time is right. We buy lemonade and find a place to sit and wait by the cool, clear stream that runs through the middle of the reservation.

The right time to begin the dance will be determined in the ancient way, by a small group of men standing on the rooftops of the tiered adobe dwellings. Their periodic ancestral calls to the elements seem to echo a question, and as we look out to the tree-covered mountain beyond the pueblo walls, our Anglo impatience for things to begin slowly diminishes.

After the Corn Dance, we meet Richard Suazo (his real name), a thirty-nine-year-old Taos artist whose gallery, Aspen Winds Indian Arts, occupies the site of his ancestral home on the southern side of the pueblo. Richard's recovery from alcohol addiction has been informed by waiting through the practice of meditation. As a schoolboy, Richard never felt he could fit in with his "perfect" Anglo classmates. The religious expectations of his parents, as well as aspects of the pueblo tradition, further alienated him. The death of both parents when he was an adolescent brought further pain, which he sought to alleviate with drugs and alcohol.

Richard's continued drinking as an adult affected his marriage and resulted in divorce. In his mid-thirties, a sense of despair about his addiction brought him to a turning point and launched an inner journey that has transformed his life. By allowing himself to experience the feelings he had always avoided through alcohol, Richard has discovered an unexpected richness in life. The beautiful and unique story-shields he creates are expressions of his growth.

This dramatic life change has brought him back full circle into the sanctuary of tribal life, where he looks forward to becoming an elder as he approaches his fortieth birthday. Awake to his experiences and feelings, Richard maintains an appreciation of his people and their traditional way of life, a life he rejected in his youth.

I had my beginnings right here in this house. This is where my parents lived as newlyweds, and they raised my older brothers and sisters in this house. My sister and I came along in my parents' forties, so we were always expected to fill our older brothers' and sisters' shoes. We were told that they had done good, and we were expected to do the exact same things.

There's a long history of many, many families living in this house. My grandfather and his brothers and their fathers before them—they have lived in this corner for centuries. They still talk about the hard things that have happened to them living here, like a smallpox epidemic that killed a lot of people. In my father's family, most all the women died. They were left with almost nothing but men. For a long time, it was mostly men who took care of each other.

My father was one of the first people to go to college from our tribe. He was a very, very intelligent person. And he had a real gentle spirit. That's what I always think about when I think about my father. My mother had a mischievous spirit, and I think that's where my artistry comes from. The good-with-your-hands part comes from my dad.

Here on the pueblo, the expectations of people are very much past-oriented. There's a pattern that everybody is supposed to follow. A man is expected to take a wife, be a good hunter, do the tribal duties, provide for his family, raise his children.

The duty of every man and every woman in this pueblo includes participating in the religious traditions of the tribe. My dad was an elder in his *kiva*, so he used to be very involved in the Indian religion here.

My parents also went to Catholic church every Sunday. They did the duty part of being a Catholic. They took all us kids to church. They had all the religious articles in the house like every Catholic should have. I grew up with that, too.

The expectations from my people about roles, and especially about religion, were very rigid. They were set. And I never felt that I was adequate.

I never felt I would live up to them. What a relief now to know that I don't have to.

We didn't have much exposure to the white culture during our childhood. We only saw the tourists who came here. As a result, when we were growing up, my sister and I often commented about how we thought the white people were always so clean and so nice. They were like perfect, really perfect, is what we thought.

Until I finished grade school—right here, within walking distance—I was in a cocoon. I never went away from here. I never had TV, so I didn't know what other people away from here did. All my lessons growing up were things that pertained to the Pueblo. I wasn't prepared for anything else. I didn't know about other people's ways until I went to junior high school in Taos.

There were a few Anglo kids in junior high school at the time, and they were pretty much like my first perception of Anglos. They seemed real perfect to me. They never made mistakes. So going to school was a very traumatic experience for me because I was not prepared for other people's values or the way they thought.

Unfortunately, at the time my defense against not fitting in was to go get into drugs and drinking—drinking, mostly. I put a buffer between myself and others by drinking and doing mind-altering substances.

My whole junior high school and high school period was very, very mixed up. I would only go to school sporadically. I would do a lot of running around with friends. At the same time, my whole family was in an upheaval. We were getting uprooted as a family because my parents' health was going down the drain. Before I finished high school, both my parents died.

I ended up not finishing high school, and I eventually went to California, which was another culture shock. I was seventeen years old. I wanted to see the world, and to me, California represented everything. Everything. I was out in California, I think, three years, then Colorado for most of ten years. When I was in Denver, I threw myself into mainstream America, doing the nine-to-five of paying the rent and working at a series of low-paying jobs.

During this period I had a son, and I got married to a woman from this tribe. Unfortunately, my alcohol use was so big in my life that I chose that over my family. As a result, I got divorced. My wife and son moved back to the pueblo. I went through about five painful years, really hitting the floor with my body every night, just trampling myself and always wondering what I had done wrong in my life to have this happen to me.

I was always avoiding the responsibility of really looking at what was going on with me, so I came back to the pueblo. I think, mainly, I came back because it was getting harder and harder to leave my son when I visited him. It was so hard to look into his eyes every time I was saying goodbye. And I knew that the time was coming when my responsibilities were not to be avoided anymore, my responsibilities to this pueblo and the clan I belong to.

It was hard to get back into living here. I didn't feel quite like I fit in, because I had been gone for ten years. I had always been trying to find a way to fit in somewhere. I was trying to feel inside the way I thought other people felt, or at least how they looked. This was what I was trying to do all that time, and it wasn't happening.

As a result, I felt like a freak and I always ran away. I never completed anything. Many, many times, I ended up almost dying of poor health because of my drinking.

The most fortunate thing in my life was that, about six years ago, I suffered mental anguish to a point where I wanted to completely turn my life around—so badly that I took myself away from the drinking.

I was influenced pretty much at that time by AA friends. I wanted my life to be like theirs. I wanted to succeed the way they had. I was just going to the meetings and not getting much out of it, but what I *was* getting was that these people loved me because I wanted to be sober, and they accepted me. They are the most genuine, human people around, just very open and honest about what we're all into. AA was there for me if I needed it. But my hunger was for something deeper.

The understanding that I got about my addiction is that my mind is addicted to alcohol, my body is addicted to it, but there is a part of me that is not addicted to it. Something in me was screaming all those years when I was abusing myself with alcohol. That part is not addicted, and if I keep in contact with that part, I will never take another drink again.

During this period, I made a real good friend who introduced me to some teachings of an Eastern holy man, Osho. What Osho was saying hit me so hard and so deep because it was what I had felt since I was a child. In his writings, Osho kept saying, "Don't believe anything I say until you experience it for yourself, and then you will find your own truth. You will find that something will change in you." So with that in me, I tackled my life the way he suggested, which was "Don't avoid pain. Let it be there."

I tackled my fear of people. I tackled my shame over what had happened in my life, my sorrow over my parents, the inadequacy I'd felt all through my life.

I learned not to avoid feelings that come up, the anger that comes up out of past experiences, the loneliness. I learned that all these emotions are normal. Everything that I had been experiencing all my life and was trying to put in a bag and throw into a corner was normal. Through the last few years, it has just been a matter of accepting all these emotions that I have been stifling all my life.

One of the greatest realizations that happened for me was that I did not have to keep living the religion that my parents put on me. That was the biggest load that was taken off my shoulders. The Catholic religion that was presented to me as a young boy was a very scary religion where they talk of hell and heaven in very vivid terms, and I grew up scared most of the time that I was a lost cause. And yet I knew deep down, even as a real young boy, that there was something beyond what the church and my parents were giving to me.

I was born very hungry for self-knowledge. So when I got into recovery, it was not very hard for me to say, "I'm shedding this old blanket of guilt, and I'm shedding this conditioning that my parents put on me. I'm becoming a new person." Because I had never seen religion work for my parents, I didn't see any of it coming to fruit. I knew that I had to find my own way, and I am slowly finding my way through meditation. I take long walks in the mountains behind the pueblo every day, just me and my dog. I walk and I meditate.

Presently, I am experimenting with aloneness. What I was taught was that you get married, you settle down, and you surround yourself with a flood of relatives and kids. Well, I am surrounded by a big family here in the tribe, but one of the most important lessons for me is to experience my aloneness. That's the last frontier to overcome.

I think loneliness in people drives them to religion, and to people who are bad for them, and into alcohol. This loneliness is something I want to get hold of. It's a scary road because you don't have anything to fall back on. You don't have anybody to reach out to.

Just the other night I was sitting up there in the mountains, and I was thinking about some bad loneliness I've been going through this past week. And I was thinking how easy it would have been for me in the past to pick up drugs or alcohol to get rid of that feeling. Or to ask Jesus to put somebody in my life to take away the loneliness. Now I know that nobody but myself can grasp at loneliness, and work with it, and pull above it. It's very scary.

But now I don't avoid it. I look at the loneliness. I tell myself, "Damn it, I am lonely right now. I want to be with somebody. I want somebody to tell me that I am precious, that I am lovable, that they need me." However, I've been through this before, and I know that these feelings don't change by somebody reinforcing me. The change has to come out of me.

The other night I was on the verge of tears. I wanted to cry. And I was sitting up there on that mountain, and all the while I'm thinking, "I am like a blind man. Because here I am surrounded with this beauty. I'm breathing clean air, I'm looking at these beautiful mountains, the sun is setting on them, they look orange, they look purple, and here I am wrapped up with my need for another person."

And so, deeper down, there's a voice telling me, "Richard, you're going to be okay. You're going to get beyond this loneliness." And I know it's my mind, my upper part, that is in need. I'm trying to recognize that. Deep down, we all carry a peace with us. Deep down we are very happy people. But because of our surface needs, we don't see it. And that's what I'm trying to get to.

My alternative is very deadly. My alternative is to go back to alcohol, and I know that I would not pull out of it if I ever went back again. So, you know, it's life and death.

I'm becoming more and more aware that my mind is full of bad memories. I'm trying to leave my past behind. The meditation I'm doing is slowly, slowly removing the veil of my conditioning from the past. Now I'm seeing a person for the person he is, a sunset for the sunset it is, a situation for what it is.

Also, I'm slowly assuming the responsibilities of becoming an elder, becoming more a part of this village. Slowly these past few years, because of my abstinence from drinking, I know that people are starting to look up to me. I can feel it. I can see it. People are starting to look at me and say, "If he can do it, I can do it." I can't tell people how to go about living their lives. I can only be a picture for them. A lot of the things that I want to say, I can't say. It's too deep. But I can act. I can be seen.

I'm starting to live now one day at a time. Even though this was told to me in AA years ago, now I'm beginning to get what it means. I want to savor every day that I have here in this village.

I welcome growing old because of how my life has changed. Turning forty is a coming of age for me because I have only bloomed in the last six years. I don't know where I was from the time I was born until six years ago. But everything that's happened since then has been toward growth.

I've never talked about this with anybody. I keep my seeking very, very private. I go up on a mountain, and I cry if I have to. I don't hide anything from myself. And because of that, my life is just going to be more growth.

I want to grow old and watch how I develop here. For example, the elders say that everything is alive here. Well, yes. It's a good thing to say, but you have to experience the life that is here. I want to get deeper into that statement.

The Buddha said that the whole world is alive if you just open your eyes and look at it. Well, I had an experience one night in the moonlight when the moon came out, and I saw the pinon trees turn to the moon, and everything around me started acting different. The wind started acting different. Even the river started sounding different. These personal experiences verify for me that I'm on the right track.

People here tell me that they sense a leadership role in me that's going to happen. They sense a strength that I didn't know I had. A lot of acceptance for me has come about because I have accepted my weaknesses. That I wasn't man enough in my earlier years—I understand that now.

The men on the pueblo have close relations with each other through clanship. It's a tradition that is centuries old. Maybe I baptize that man's child, and for life we are bonded that way. Maybe my sister married a man, and we have that bond through my sister.

I hear all the time about the drumming groups and the men's groups that Anglo men form. I think a lot of times here we take it for granted that men can be close. It makes me really appreciate what we have here. It's like having a lot of brothers around you.

Here, you don't just go up and put your arms around another man and say, "I'm glad you're my friend." We do it in a roundabout way. We might say, "Oh, let me take that for you and fix it for you." This is what I observe in our male clanship.

The camaraderie among men here is serious because we share hardships with each other. It even takes on a bigger role when we're involved in something that's for the common good of the tribe, like a hunt.

I have many friends here, but my best friend is about twenty-five years older than I am. This man happens to be my best friend because he has the best sense of humor of any human I know. For me, that does it. That's the friendship there.

Our elders keep telling us that life is about hardship and laughter. And one thing that I notice in our tribe is this big sense of humor. Two of us, three of us get together and laugh about something simple. This laughter says, "Instead of driving this thing on and on, let's joke, let's release what's inside of us." This is what I have observed among my people.

After a certain age, people in the tribe get to be called "father" or "mother" by a lot of people who aren't their kids. We just call a man *thama*. That means "Father." Or *chaa*, "mother." We address older people by these names because that is the role they have taken. When you say those words to somebody, it gives you a comforting feeling. They are simple words, but they strike deep within you when you can call somebody that.

You see the kindness in these people. They have a real gruff exterior, but if you have been around them in your time of need, they are some of the most giving and loving people you can know. I cannot say enough about how this tradition of our people is in place here. You never turn somebody away. You are always there for somebody in their time of need or when somebody appears in sorrow. Hospitality is a way of life. It's a pueblo tradition.

In my younger days, I think I was not so aware of these traditions. I was always looking at my own troubles. Now I'm beginning to realize that it's a blessing to have this many people around you who care, who are concerned, who just give a word of encouragement here and there. You feel that.

There was a period of time when I was wondering what I was going to do with myself on the pueblo to make my life work. Five years ago yesterday, I opened the doors of my shop with my nephew who is a painter. I was really scared. I thought I was going to make a fool out of myself. I thought I was going to be the laughingstock of the tribe.

We had a little table here, and we did all our work on that. The first year, we just barely made it selling our own stuff. Somewhere around in the second year, the words "wholesale," "retail," "profit," and "loss" started sinking into me.

Last year, because of a small fire we had, it really hit me how much a brothers' and sisters' co-op this shop has become. I realized this shop is not just about me anymore. It is about forty or fifty different artists who have their work in here. It has to do with the fact that we are all taking care of each other, taking care of each other's needs. That is what this shop has become. I want this shop to honor each piece from each artist that comes in here.

I have found that, as a creative person, you have to be content with what you're doing. When you're making a particular piece, you have to be happy working with that stone or clay or canvas. If the happiness is not there, you will not create what you want to create.

My art is story-shields that I make with different stuff, like animal skins, feathers, branches, and natural pigment colors. My art has a lot to do with my growth. It has to do with the things that I want to say that I can't put into words. So the hard work is coming out with a message, with a teaching, with a treasure that I have found that I want to pass on to people. My art and my growth—it's the same thing.

One example of how my story-shields teach through art is a shield that I recently gave to the medical clinic here. A couple of years ago, we had some of the worst snow we had ever had in our area. People were complaining about how miserable and cold the snow was. I was starting to fall into that trap. I was starting to complain along with them.

Then I went walking up in the canyon, and it started to snow again. Those snowflakes started coming down real slowly. Have you ever seen snowflakes that fall real silent? They would come down, and they would hit the rocks or the earth, and they would just be there for an instant, and then they would be gone.

I started thinking, "This is one of the most beautiful things I have ever witnessed in life. This is art. This is nature's art. Snow is a miracle."

I realized that although we may sleep through it, life is a miracle. And I carried that insight, that instant with me for about a year-and-a-half. And when they asked me to make one of my shields for the clinic, I knew that insight had to be the subject for the shield. I named it "The Miracle Is Here."

I have found that my openness about life brings me so many rewards that wouldn't have happened if I had sheltered myself and stuck to one religion and the addiction I had.

Life is about having a child within you all the time. Life is a spiritual experience every day. I read a bumper sticker the other day. You have probably seen it. It said, "It's never too late to have a happy childhood." I believe that very much. And I accept that there is a child within me who needs to experience life again, except this time he's not unhappy.

He Did It His Way

Mike Fitz

The first six weeks after I was laid off, I was taking it all personally. I had lost my identity. After six weeks of struggling with that, I woke up one day and thought, "You are not the job. The job isn't you." I had confused my job with my life, my person. How many times do we say, "What do you do?" when we meet someone for the first time? Men ask this. It's not the same as asking who you are.

Job loss is a major concern for many men in the '90s as corporations downsize in order to stay solvent. For men in midlife, the sudden undervaluation of their accumulated knowledge and experience can be crushing. As Frank Pittman writes in Man Enough: Fathers, Sons, and the Search for Masculinity, *"When we lose our work, we lose our dignity, our network, our purpose, our structure, and we live in a state of shame."*

These words could have been written expressly for Mike Fitz, a fifty-five-year-old unemployed sales representative. Nothing in the messages he received growing up prepared him for the current economic climate of widespread corporate layoffs. Like other men of his era, Mike was raised on the promise that hard work and loyalty would guarantee success and mark him as a man.

As Mike reflects on his life, he recognizes how such messages, delivered in adolescence, led to confusion regarding his early career decisions. Likewise, familial and societal messages about how men need to stay in control of their feelings shaped Mike's need to dominate his marriage. Mike raised his three young children following a divorce when he was thirty-nine. He went to counseling, where he was able to grieve the loss of his marriage and reassess his motivations.

Now, having unexpectedly lost his job, he has joined a support group of other midlife men who are out of work. There he has learned to be more open about his feelings and to offer encouragement to other men who, like him, have faced a loss of identity along with the loss of a job. Being in trusting relationships with other men has helped him develop a sense of being more than just a breadwinner.

In spite of a heart attack several years ago, Mike frequently smokes cigarettes as we sit at his dining room table one snowy winter morning. He is still in the process of coming to terms with the changes in his life. His anger and sense of betrayal occasionally come to the surface.

On the other hand, the close relationships Mike enjoys within his new family sustain him. The roles of father, husband, and friend provide him with the sense of purpose that, in the past, only work could give him. He is learning, finally, to take life as it comes.

I had a great childhood. We didn't have TV, but I remember enjoying the radio. I also read a lot. And I enjoyed the freedom of being able to do for myself—like getting out in the alley after school and playing a game of football.

There was one particular Boy Scout troop leader that I really looked up to. He had a job and his own family, but he would involve himself in our activities a lot more than many of our own fathers would. My friends and I really respected him. We were grateful to him.

Some of the lessons we learned at that age probably didn't serve us too well later on. Like "Men don't cry." "Be tough." "The good guys always win." "Play by the rules or suffer the consequences." There were no shades of grey. You didn't bend the rules.

As we got into junior high school, many of the guys I hung around with got interested in athletics. Here was a new dimension to playing by the rules. We were the gladiators. We were expected to be strong. Be *something*. Be of good character.

Being the oldest of six kids ... My folks were very loving and devoted, I don't want to give the wrong impression about that, but they gave me the sense that, because I was the oldest, I had to set the example. After a while, I got tired of it.

I made a decision my senior year. I had spent a number of summers in high school working as a counselor at a Knights of Columbus camp. I made friends with some of the older counselors who were in the seminary studying to be priests. So I thought I'd give seminary a try.

After high school, I entered the seminary, and I was there for maybe two months, and I thought, "This is not really what I want." But I stuck to it for a whole year. It was that old hang-in-there thing. I think my mom and dad, as Catholic parents, were proud as hell, and I didn't want to let them down. And that began a long siege of people-pleasing. I learned to play that game.

I left the seminary after a year and started college. A good private school, very academic. Halfway through, I decided I wanted to try teaching, so I declared a major in education. But my father had picked the school, and it got a little too rigorous for me. Most of my friends who were in college at other places were having a real swinging time.

I turned twenty-one just before my sophomore year, and I figured, "I'm going to declare myself emancipated. I'm going to transfer on my own." My father said to me, "If you're going to be emancipated, you're going to pay for it." So I said fine.

My game plan was to drop out for a year and earn some money and transfer to a state school. It was that feeling of "I'm free. I want to do it my way." All around me people were offering advice, but I chose not to take it.

Within a year of that decision, I found myself married to someone from my hometown. She was a few years younger than me. We had to elope because her father was not about to put up with her leaving college to marry the likes of me. He was not strong on Catholics. And of course, she was underage. So we had to go out of state to get married. She was working. I was working half days, going to school half days.

When our first child was born, we hired a full-time baby sitter. I had to work two different jobs. But I was doing it my way. This began to hurt our families, especially our mothers, because it was almost a year and a half before we went back home for a visit. I think there was some bitterness on my part, too, over the fact that I hadn't been welcomed into my wife's family as the great white knight. Still, I was doing it *my* way.

My wife was also someone who had wanted to get away from her home. I think for both of us it was more a sense of wanting to make the break than a sense of being in this marriage for a lifetime. That happened to a lot of people in those days.

It was not a good marriage although it lasted seventeen years. I was in a lot of denial at the end, and it took me years to realize that I had to point the finger at myself. I had to take my share of the blame. But however we felt about the marriage, it didn't prevent us from producing offspring. We had three kids in six-and-a-half years. And it took me ten straight quarters to graduate. I was working twenty to thirty hours a week.

I started teaching, which is what I had set out to do. Again, in the sense of "I'll be all right if I do my job. I'll create a successful life if I keep my nose to the grindstone. This is a noble calling."

I was a good teacher. I really enjoyed it. What I resented about it was that my peers who had graduated in other areas were enjoying more affluent lifestyles. But rather than admit I wanted a better lifestyle, rather than making a change, I stayed with it. I wanted to appear to be the success at teaching that I had set out to be.

I really got resentful about the money and about the fact that I wasn't thinking for myself. After my third year of teaching, it was a very easy decision to get the heck out. I had developed this attitude that "Well, by gosh, others are out there getting theirs, so I'm going to get mine." That attitude wasn't really me. Rather, it was the me I thought I had to be if I was a success. It was a good defense mechanism, this feeling of "I gotta prevail, I gotta do it."

So I went into the thing I had never wanted to go into. Sales. I had fought that notion ever since I was in high school. I remember one of my dad's friends saying, "With your gift of the gab, you'll be a great salesman." I thought, "Who wants to be a salesman? Who wants to go around pursuing people that way?" Sales isn't really like that, but that was the way I perceived it.

I got into the book publishing business in 1967, into one of the big-three companies in publishing. Well, talk about feeding the ego. We were to dress a certain way and present ourselves a certain way, and I bought into that. That was class. I thought, "Now I have purpose in my life." It was a good living, but in the back of my mind I always had the feeling that I wasn't doing what I really wanted to do, that I had left teaching out of spite.

It became apparent after about five or six years that sales is…well, sales. I realized I was doing the same thing year in, year out. Doing well at it, but it was like the Peggy Lee song "Is That All There Is?"

My wife had not worked since after the third child was born, and she was getting antsy now that all the kids were in school. She made a decision to get back into the work force. I had no objection to that, as long as the kids were taken care of when I wasn't there.

But then her outside job began to interfere with her time at home, and that led to a serious resentment on my part. Again, I needed to be in control. We had to be doing it my way. "Our way" had to be my way. I admit that. I have no problem with admitting that now. In my forties, I did.

Today I can see how she would want to get out and see something and be something and do something. Because she was not even twenty when we got married. She spent a large part of her young adulthood being subservient, not so much out of a sense of respect for our marriage, or for me, just for the sake of survival.

And within two years…Boy! The marriage just disintegrated. And it was tough. We had a girl who was a junior in high school, my middle son was in the ninth grade, and the little girl was in seventh grade.

When the marriage started to crumble, I told my wife, "If this is what you want, you go get it. But you're not going to take the kids with you and make them start from the bottom." One of my closest friends said, "Do you realize what you're saying? If she takes you up on that, you've got to raise those three kids."

I said, "That's the way it's going to be. I'm not going to have them go with her. We've got a comfortable home here. Their friends are here. If she's the one that wants out, she's going to go alone."

I thought that would call her bluff, that she would come back to my way of thinking and I would become less resentful, that we would compromise. But she said, "Okay. I'm gone."

The fear hit me about six days after she moved out. Like, "What do I do? How the heck am I going to pull this off?" I started to fall apart within a month. But I wasn't going to let her—or her family, or my family—know it. Most of all, I didn't want the kids to see it. But the kids *were* seeing it. And I was thinking, "Everything's cool."

We had spent three months seeing a counselor, about a year before the marriage ended, just to see if we could do something. I had been thinking maybe this guy could talk some sense into her. After the divorce, I ended up going back to him.

I was a bag of jelly when I hit the counselor's office. "Grown men don't cry," yet I would cry in this guy's office. I stayed with him for almost a year.

I was thirty-nine. I got to thinking about the big four-O coming. I remembered all the crazy parties we'd have with our neighbors and friends when they turned forty. And some of it was cruel, some of the stuff we would do to these guys. And I knew my turn was coming.

About this time, I had an opportunity to transfer to another state. I thought, "I'm going to take the geographical cure." I took a job offer with another smaller company, and it turned out to be a good job. I was getting my way again. I got the hell out of Pennsylvania right after my daughter graduated from high school.

But geographical cures don't always work, because you take something with you. Yourself. I remember it being so hard on my younger son and daughter. She was just entering ninth grade, and that's a rough time. But we did it.

The third day after the moving truck left, the Welcome Wagon lady showed up. And she wants to meet the misses. She sat there and gave me her spiel, and after twenty minutes I finally said, "I'm a single parent." Her first assumption is that I'm a widower. I said, "No, I'm divorced." And it was like she couldn't get out of there quick enough.

There was a stigma attached to me. And the two youngest were stigmatized at school. People said, "You're living with your father?" So it was a little hard on them. But I had done it my way.

I was about six months into the new job when I met my present wife. She was divorced. We dated most of that year. Then I asked her if she wanted to get married, and she said, "Yes." I couldn't believe it. She's twelve years younger than I am. I thought that was a chasm. She just seemed so much different from people my age. Of course, she didn't have children, and that was refreshing. She didn't have any war stories to compare with mine.

She was like fresh air to me, and she seemed to get along with my kids right off the bat. It wasn't until a year after we were married that I got to see that there was some resentment on the part of the two kids who were still living at home. They never had had any counseling, and I look back and wonder now if I did wrong by not getting them some.

I didn't know until they were both out of high school that they were suffering over "What did we do wrong that caused the divorce?" In those years, they were going through the same kind of denial. I was the type of person who would pull the veil down and not let you really know what I was feeling. And they did the same thing, so what was I to think? I'm in denial. I don't see their denial. I'm thinking everything's cool.

"You having a good time, kids?"

"Yeah."

"Give me a hug. Love ya."

"Love ya."

Boom. Boom.

About three years into the marriage, my wife said, "One child. Please?" We had never talked about it before. She was now in her thirties. I said, "That's do-able."

Jamie was born in '84. Boy, I'll tell you, that was an experience. What a hoot! And I took some ribbing about it because I was almost forty-five when he was born.

Then, when Jamie was just two, my wife became pregnant again. That really shook me because I had had a heart attack in late '84—Jamie wasn't quite a year old yet. I felt lost that summer I found out my wife was pregnant again. There was never any thought of bailing out or abortion or anything like that, but I got very fearful.

We had Kathleen then, and that taught me something. No one had taught me how to be a parent to the first three kids, and I didn't have time in my twenties to pay much attention. But with these two, I had an awareness of them as little people, of being part of the whole process, watching them grow up.

I'm different with these two than I was when I was twenty. I don't have the same expectations of them as I did of the other three. I've been around a number of years, and I'm seeing things differently. My God, I shouldn't say "differently"—I'm seeing things for the first time. I have the ability to give my two younger children something. My feelings.

I was furloughed from my job in '90—a "permanent layoff," they called it. I had just turned fifty. I spent six solid months trying to get back in publishing and found out they're not hiring people my age. This time I didn't get resentful. I got scared. "What am I going to do now with these two coming up?"

I got into this independent sales line, but the drawback there was that, to make the kind of money I would like to make, I'd have had to do a lot of traveling and invest a lot of my own capital into building up some territories. I didn't want to jeopardize the investments I'd made toward my retirement. Besides, it's a rough way to make a living, especially if you're working strictly on commission.

This was all taking its toll, so I said, "Who needs the aggravation? The stress?" I just packed it in. I gave all the companies I was representing ninety days' notice.

So here I am. Coming up on fifty-five and still haven't landed anything permanent. But I don't have that sense of panic now. A group of us who have been laid off started meeting informally, on a weekly basis, not so much to commiserate about our lives but just to let each other know "There's somebody out there like you." We're there for each other, so that I can go home at the end of the day and look my wife in the eye and myself in the mirror and say, "Don't take it personal, buddy. You're not alone."

I've seen losing a job devastate men my age. And I know it could do that to me if I let it. So here's where I have some control. Don't get me wrong—there are days when I say, "Aw, shit. Why bother?" But it's not a permanent thing, and it hasn't destroyed me.

I have learned about what my self-destructive and resentful mind can do. I've seen it play havoc. Fortunately, I had already experienced it during the divorce. I guess having had some counseling in dealing with it, and remembering how I felt about what I did to myself at that time, has helped me with where I am now.

The kids in my family weren't raised to ask for help. I loved my mom, but, if they ever name a patron saint of people who stuff feelings, it'll be her, Saint Loretta. "Don't let Uncle Jack see." "Don't tell Aunt Norma." Because it might upset somebody.

But when you're ten years old, and your top is ready to blow, what do you do? You get in trouble for getting angry. So I was taught not to trust my feelings.

You were mentioning earlier about how girls tend to talk to each other. Guys didn't do that. Or we did, but it was never about feelings. It was about goals. We were talking about what our place in the world was going to be. Goals. Achievements. Competition.

Today, men are sharing more with one another, and I feel comfortable with that. That's something I've noticed over the last five or six years, guys fifty and up facing the same kinds of disappointments. There's a lot of talk among men about things we wouldn't have talked about twenty years ago.

It's good for me to know the people in my group. It was sad seeing four men that I had known for a long time die prematurely, one of them a suicide. But I can weigh that against those who have had an awakening in their lives. And I don't have to feel alone. I don't have to feel trapped and beaten up. I've learned that I don't have to prove anything to anybody in order to survive.

The first six weeks after I was laid off, I was taking it all personally. I had lost my identity. After six weeks of struggling with that, I woke up one day and thought, "You are not the job. The job isn't you." I had confused my job with my life, my person. How many times do we say, "What do you do?" when we meet someone for the first time? Men ask this. It's not the same as asking who you are.

The people I'm most comfortable with now are in their fifties and sixties—people who have come to the same comfort level I have after the heart-wrenching experience of being dumped out of the marketplace. The ones who say, "Why not just see where life goes from here?"

Crafting a Life

Dean Lewis

> I began to think about the deeper things of life, mankind and God and the creation around me. The two important questions in life, I think, are "Who am I?" and "What am I doing here?" I slowly began to develop a personal philosophy of life. I was in my forties.

Dean Lewis, a fifty-five-year-old school maintenance worker and homesteader, more or less stumbled into a midlife change that thoroughly suits him. A move in his late thirties for practical reasons became an adventure in a rugged area of West Virginia. Dean left a job he loved behind in New Jersey and, in true pioneer tradition, moved west and single-handedly built a home for his family in the remote woods.

In his forties, after going through a divorce, Dean began the gradual process of piecing together the scraps of his life that still had strong personal meaning to him. A year spent living alone proved a fertile time for him to meditate and clarify his values. Dean's long fascination with religion and spirituality, his boyhood interest in handicrafts, and his love of simple living (developed as a boy visiting his grandparents' farm in Vermont) slowly came together to form a well-integrated life.

Dean greets us as we pull up in front of his log home—a relief to us after a somewhat harrowing drive on the deeply rutted road off the main highway that leads to his house. It is quiet in these hills except for the occasional barking of the family dog and a gunshot announcing the beginning of hunting season.

We leave our shoes at the door and take a sock-footed tour of the house. Dean's wife, Ruth, has fixed tea for us. Dean is clearly proud of this warm, inviting house that he built from the ground up, with its hardwood floors and its many windows that bring in the surrounding woods. A bathroom floor has been done with refinished slate blackboards from an old school house, a special touch that demonstrates Dean's creativity.

Evidence of Dean and Ruth's joy in crafts is everywhere. Ruth's prize-winning quilts cover the beds and walls. One of Dean's stained-glass windows, an owl with outstretched wings, hangs in the living room. Another window in the kitchen features a stork poised for flight. Both pieces seem so alive we can almost hear the sound of flapping wings.

I was born and grew up in New Jersey. My mom was an interior decorator. As a young woman from a fairly well-to-do family, she had left home to put herself through three years of interior decorating school. She lived in the city, in her own apartment, and supported herself. So she was a rebel, although in a constructive way. My dad was an automobile mechanic with his own business.

I remember the day World War II ended. My mother was in tears. Dad came home early that day. They embraced and danced around the kitchen. I don't know how old I was, maybe five.

My parents decided it would be a good thing for me if they moved to the country, so they bought a farm in a rural area of New Jersey. My father's father had a farm in Vermont that we used to visit every summer. To me, it was paradise, a place heated exclusively with wood, with all the cooking done on an enormous wood stove. No electricity. No telephones. Lots of home-canned goods. Subsistence living at its best.

I remember riding with my grandfather in the wagon to town, the stories he'd tell me. And the clip-clopping of the horses. And the whole idea that a lot of the things he had there on the farm had been made by him. I liked the idea of making things.

Once, when I was a kid, my mother had a little electric mixer, and the cord came apart right where the plug was. I said, "I can fix that." I really didn't know how, but I figured I could do it. When my father came home, he looked it over and said, "I couldn't do better myself." I felt like a million bucks. It was wonderful. Worth a lot to me.

I enjoyed the country until I was fourteen years old; then my parents moved back to the city. I guess their financial situation had slowly gone downhill. I'm sure there was no work for my mom out there. I know she didn't leave the house very often to do decorating work. My dad worked in a garage and came home tired and greasy every night.

When we moved back into the city, my mom gave me a lot of freedom. On Saturdays, a friend of mine and I would take the train near Newark to Hoboken. We'd buy a ferry ticket, go across the Hudson River, and get off at the 14th Street ferry dock in Manhattan. It was an adventure—the train ride, the boat ride, then walking the streets of New York until it started to get dark, when we'd make it back to the ferry dock and reverse the process.

In the city, we'd go into the fish markets, and we'd go into the vegetable markets, and we'd go into the garment district. I felt very much at home in the garment district. We'd meet Hasidic Jews, with their black hats and beards, and I felt in tune with their way of doing things.

I think one of the turning points in my thinking, as far as making things with my hands goes, came when I was running on the track team in high school. One day I just made up my mind I wasn't going to run anymore for the team. Because I had never really liked sports. Team sports seemed especially silly to me. All that energy and expense, and for what?

I told my track coach, "I'm quitting the team." He was horrified. I said, "I don't want to chase balls around the field, or myself around the track, anymore. I'm a maker, not a player." And he couldn't understand it.

After I graduated from high school, I enlisted in the Air Force for four years, which gave me a chance to travel around and see different places. I was stationed on a base in California. I was a nineteen-year-old and really naive.

One day, I was in the control tower fixing radio equipment, and I looked out over this field of bombers. They were flying in and out every day. I saw this large truck with a white cover pull down off a hill. It pulled in underneath one of these bombers.

I was curious about that, and I asked one of the control-tower operators, "What are they doing there?" He said, "They're loading weapons. Every plane that goes out of here has six hundred bombs on board. And we go out and fly around near Russia, just circling in the air."

I started to think about those bombers, and about the idea of war. Do we really need it? I became more and more of a peacenik. Became more outspoken about it. Got in more and more trouble. Although I was honorably discharged, it was not a good thing between me and the military.

After that, I got to spend a year in Alaska, which was a total delight. I lived in a place called King Salmon, a place where there are salmon canneries at the mouth of a pretty good-sized river, right at the beginning of the Aleutian chain.

A very dear friend wanted me to stay and open a restaurant in Anchorage with him. But Anchorage was too citified for me. I wanted to be out in the country. My dad was sick at that time, and I hadn't been home in two-and-a-half years. I was tired of wandering, so I decided to go back east for a while.

That summer, my dad died after a three-year bout with cancer. I had been shielded from that. My parents had had some kind of pact—he would never talk to her about it, and she would never talk to him about it. They pretended they didn't know about the cancer. But my dad made more and more frequent visits to the hospital, and finally passed away. I was really blessed to be there to hold him in my arms when he died.

I had been married shortly before his death. We bought a house in a large wilderness area in New Jersey, the Pine Barrens, where there are small lakes and streams, and these funny little stunted pine trees go on for miles and miles. A true wilderness. My daughter was born there.

I became interested in work that was being done nearby in a machine shop, which was attached to the electronics research lab I worked in. I began to watch the machinists and get interested in how they made things, pick up some ideas about machine-shop technology and technique. I was fascinated by the idea of working with metal.

So I left my job in electronics and went to work as an industrial model-maker, making one-of-a-kind prototypes of everything. I actually enjoyed getting up in the morning and going to work, because it was like a hobby that I got paid for doing. I had all the tools and all the equipment I wanted, and other model-makers to work with.

My family had several years of real happy living in New Jersey. But we saw our local taxes going up and up, so we started looking for another place to live. Every summer we'd use up our vacation time camping in West Virginia and looking for property. And we'd go home disappointed.

Finally, we found these twelve acres of woods, and we just fell in love with the place. It was on a river and had a spring where we could get our drinking water. We put our house up for sale and bought the land. Lived in a little shack nearby. But the rent was so cheap—thirty dollars a month. I started clearing the property, cutting trees and enlarging the circle from the central spot where the house is now, until we had about an acre cleared. I tried to be selective and save the most beautiful trees.

When I first came here, the plan was that I would work on the house full-time and get it built. Because, after talking with some builders, we figured that about half the cost of building a house is labor. But my wife developed a problem with cancer and was not able to hold a regular job. So it fell to me to build the house *and* hold down a job.

When I came to West Virginia, of course, there was no call for anything like a prototype model-maker. But I also had had four years of training as a machinist in New Jersey, so I thought I would try to find a job doing that here. But no one needed a machinist. Several places where I had applied didn't even know what a machinist was. That was really depressing.

I determined that I would take the first job that appeared, and when I was offered a job as a maintenance person at a local county school, I thought, "Well, I can do that. It isn't what I'm trained to do, it isn't what I like to do, but I can do it." I saw it as an alternative to working in an office or doing something else I really hated.

It's the sort of a job that can support my craft-work habit. That's the only thing I can say about it. It isn't very rewarding, and it doesn't pay that well. But it is steady, and that's something in West Virginia. Work is really scarce here.

About a year later, my daughter moved away to the city. And the relationship with my wife had been steadily going downhill. I guess it was differences in temperament that contributed to the slow breakup of our marriage. Finally, we decided to divorce.

I lived alone in the house for a year. I had never lived alone in my life. I worked my regular job, and I came home. For some reason, I had imagined that I would have lots of freedom, lots of free time to pursue my crafts.

What I found out was that I had *no* freedom. Because now I had to do all the cooking, all the laundry, all the bookwork, all the maintenance, plus my job. I didn't have time for my crafts at all. So I was pretty disillusioned.

During that time, a lot of the things my mom had taught me came back to me. She had taught me how to do some basic cooking. She had insisted that I learn how to do laundry, clean house. She had said, "Someday you'll thank me for this."

And the day came when I was thanking her for it. The values that my mom had given me became a lot more focused after I was by myself. And even though I was busy with physical things, I found more and more time to think and meditate. Things my dad had done and said came back to me, too, became more valuable to me. I saw the wisdom of both my parents' teachings.

I was at a turning point in my life. My spiritual life became more focused. When I worked in the garden, I'd be praying openly, talking to God. I began to think about the deeper things of life, mankind and God and the natural creation around me. The two important questions in life,

I think, are "Who am I?" and "What am I doing here?" I slowly began to develop a personal philosophy of life. I was in my forties.

I had always enjoyed gardening. I tried to support myself on as little money as I possibly could. I saw that I'd be better off, both financially and health-wise, if I ate as much out of my garden as possible. So I did as much organic gardening as I could. I read a lot about health problems related to food. I became an environmentally conscious person.

All this was developing while I was living alone, which was a wonderful time for me, a kind of monastic time. I just kept wanting more and more to live here by myself. I continued to garden and think for a year. I had also decided I wanted to live a celibate life for that time. I didn't date or go out anywhere or have any companionship other than my work.

Near the end of my time of living alone, I went with a very good friend to a Scottish music concert over in Charleston, West Virginia. It was the first time I'd been out of the county in nine months. At intermission time, as we were standing in the hall drinking a cup of coffee, this lady came by me wearing a long skirt and boots and a neat-looking vest. She could have been a gypsy queen. I was immediately attracted to her.

I have never been very bold or forward in my relations with ladies, but I kind of half put out my hand and asked her to stop. I said, "I know you from somewhere." Then I realized what a dorky statement that was. But she did stop, and we talked. And I really liked her.

She invited me to go to a party after the concert. Well, I hadn't been to a party in years. I was really coming out of the woods. I'd lost any polish I may have had when it came to being with people. But it was okay. She and I sat on the back porch of this old house in Charleston and talked until three in the morning.

Ruth lived in a small apartment with her two sons, in the same county as I did. She taught in the local high school. So I really *had* seen her before! I found out that she was a craftsperson and really loved to work with her hands. We started dating. Not going anywhere, just visiting each other. It was very exciting to make a new friend. We started developing a real love for each other.

I was determined not to plunge into any deep relationship. I didn't want it to develop into a romance if I could help it. But I couldn't help it. Love happens. It was only a matter of weeks after we started getting serious that I asked Ruth to marry me.

About this same time, I started developing another important part of me, which was my spiritual life. Seemed like all the things I'd believed and known about started to come into focus. I had been exposed to many religions growing up back in New Jersey. And I had studied them, not in a formal way, but on my own. I had always thought of myself as "incurably religious." I had studied Zen Buddhism. And I had always been fascinated by the Old Testament.

Ruth belonged to a religion called the Bahai faith, so I talked with her about it. I began to understand more and more about what the Bahai faith teaches about God's desire for the world. And it fit in exactly with what I already believed. Or rather, I fit into it. I now feel a great peace within this faith.

So Ruth and I were married. This was in 1986. And that's basically it. Ruth and I have been close companions ever since. We share a common faith in God and, pretty much, common goals. We try to keep the kids living a moral and creative lifestyle.

Another area of my life that brings me contentment now is making things with my hands. I have done some wood-carving, a lot of craft work—stained glass, silver jewelry, knives, just playing around with a lot of different things. Finding out how things are made is almost an obsession with me.

When Ruth and I get off work Friday night, it's crafts time until Monday morning. A lot of times I'll take the kids, and we'll go for a bike ride to give Ruth some space to do her lace-making. Or Ruth will go do something and take the kids and leave me an afternoon free to do what I want. We try really hard to give each other space in our lives. It's not a matter of "letting" or "permitting." It's just giving each other the space and time to do what we want to do.

One of the White Hats

Keith Hecker

> I would say that our generation's view of a man was prob-
> ably of someone who went out and worked hard every
> day, took his family to the grocery store on Friday nights,
> maybe to the drive-in on Saturday nights once a month,
> church on Sundays, back to work on Monday...But by the
> time our generation reached twenty, the innocence that
> we had known as kids was gone because of the Vietnam
> war and how our society had changed so much because
> of the war.

*We meet Keith Hecker on a cold day in midwinter. He parks his grey pickup
truck in front of a mutual friend's home and comes in shedding a heavy
parka, gloves, and scarf. He complains about how the cold bothers the plates
in his back, although he looks fit enough with his high barrel chest and
square shoulders. His short, medium-brown hair is parted in the middle, and
he wears round wire-framed glasses. He has a soft, raspy voice colored with
a Midwestern accent. We settle down to talk over cups of black coffee.*

*At forty-five, Keith is three years into a social work degree, which he
plans to use to create a position as a Veteran's Administration coordinator
for Native American veterans living on reservations in Arizona. He now
sees this job as his life's work. Discovering this career goal at midlife was the
result of a long process of redefining his identity as a worker and a warrior.*

*Keith's story captures what it was like for men who grew up in the '50s,
an era in which it was possible to believe in the romance of wars and
heroes, the unquestioned authority of fathers, and the availability of jobs
for people who wanted them. His experiences in the '70s and '80s—including a nine-year stint in the Navy SEALS in Vietnam, two failed marriages,
and serious back injuries—forced him to question long-held assumptions,
many about manhood, as he entered his forties.*

*The realization that his broken spine could have killed or paralyzed him
awoke Keith to a sense of unfulfilled purpose. He began to search for answers.
The first clue jumped off a page in an occupational handbook and, despite his
frustration with education when he was a teenager, led him to the college
classroom. His volunteer work at a local Native American center, intended to*

test his new career goal, uncovered more about his personal abilities.
Feeling good about who he is has allowed Keith to trust himself in a per-
sonal relationship again. He is three years into a secure and happy marriage
with a woman he calls his closest friend.

Midlife has brought Keith important new insights and resolutions. As a
warrior turned peace-giver, Keith retains his strong work ethic and now
plans to apply it to helping others overcome difficulties he once faced.

I was born August 7, 1950. My father was a truck driver. My mother was a
housewife who occasionally worked out of the home at different kinds of
jobs. I was an only child, but fortunately I had a lot of cousins, so I was
never lonely. We moved quite a bit because, dad being a truck driver there,
weren't a whole lot of high-paying jobs, so we had to go where the money
was.

In 1956, we moved to Middle Bass Island in Lake Erie. That was my first
year of school. It was a one-room schoolhouse. The winters were pretty
rough because it was all open territory. They had these old Model A and
Model T trucks. They'd put chains on the tires and go across the ice to the
mainland for groceries.

I never played any organized sports until I was about eleven years old.
If they had asked me how to shingle a roof or mix mortar or the basics of
laying brick, I knew this stuff. I didn't know how to throw a baseball or
hit or catch. A lot of kids made fun of me for that, but you could see their
parents going, "That kid knows how to do *that?* How does he know *that?*"

I always felt like my dad was like a demi-god. What dad said went,
period. You didn't argue. You didn't question. That's the way it was done
then. Dad didn't have to ask you your opinion on anything, because he
already knew the answer.

I remember the images of parenting we saw in shows like *Ozzie and
Harriet, My Three Sons, Father Knows Best.* I could never talk to my dad that
way. I was afraid to talk to him the way kids on TV talked to their dads.

I graduated from high school in 1968. I thought I was fortunate to get
out of there. I hated school with a passion. I look at it now, and I think
that the driving force was the way I grew up. My parents were both hard-
working, and I saw both my grandfathers working day in, day out, seven
days a week. That's all I knew.

Our generation's view of a man was of someone who went out and
worked hard every day, took his family to the grocery store on Friday

nights, maybe to the drive-in on Saturday nights once a month, church on Sundays, back to work Monday. And it used to be a man had to stand up for what he thought was right, regardless. Always wore a white hat. Only the bad guys wore black hats.

But by the time our generation reached twenty, the innocence that we had known as kids was gone because of the Vietnam war and how our society had changed so much because of the war.

I joined the Navy in 1969. I had always liked that Navy uniform, and bell bottoms were in at that time. See, that's two birds with one stone. I could be in style and be in the Navy, too.

My company commander in boot camp was a Navy SEAL, and he volunteered me for SEAL training. I didn't know, at the time, what SEAL teams were. That's how naive I was. Hell, when I went in the Navy I was still a virgin.

We had to qualify with pistols and rifles as part of our training. I shot the highest in the company, rifle and pistol. My grandfather had taught me to shoot and hunt.

When I went to San Diego and started SEAL training, they told us every day, "If you don't like it here, all you have to do is ring that bell and you're out of here. You're back out to a ship somewhere, swabbing decks the rest of your life. You don't have to be here."

Well, I guess there was enough moxie in me from my parents and my grandparents that there was no way I was going to ring that bell. I don't care, I can break my leg, but I'm not ringing that bell. I think growing up watching John Wayne movies had a lot to do with making me think I could be a SEAL, be the best. The big hero—he comes home, he gets the girl. All the romance of war.

SEALs wear many hats, but basically they're used for reconnaissance on enemy units, gathering information, developing maps, rescue operations, undersea work, all kinds of diving, demolitions. My job with them was mainly as a scout.

In 1971, I went to Vietnam. I thought I had it all. I was right where I wanted to be. After the initial shock of realizing that your life could be over at any time, you tend not to focus too much on what lies ahead of you. It's the here and now that's important.

I guess I focused too much on the here and now. I just kept staying. I mean, I had originally intended to go in and do my four years, get out, come home, and start the American Dream. It didn't work out that way.

I stayed in the service all through the '70s. Didn't have any other prospects. In 1973, I took a thirty-day leave prior to reenlisting. I came home. First I went to the police department, had my service record with me. They said, "We don't have anything for you. We can't help you."

Then I went down the hall to the county sheriff's. They told me they didn't have anything that suited my job qualifications. I went to the high-way patrol. This lieutenant there said, "Your eyesight's too bad."

I never will forget that. It was on a Monday morning, and I had had enough of this runaround. I slammed my hand down on the desk. I said, "Lieutenant, I want you to think a minute. Do you know where I was last Wednesday night?" He said, "No."

I said, "Well, I can tell you. I was lying in the Mekong Delta at two o'clock in the morning to run an ambush. And you're telling me my eye-sight's too bad." He said, "I'm sorry, we don't have anything." I said, "You know what I think the problem is? I think you're afraid to take a chance on somebody like me." He denied it. I said, "Bull!" and turned around and walked out.

A week later, I got on a plane and went to the compound in Virginia and reenlisted. Like I said, I thought I had it all in the Navy.

Then, in May of '78, I had my first back operation. I had a tumor the size of a golf ball on my spine. I couldn't straighten up, and I'd lost all the feeling in my left leg. If I didn't watch how I walked, I would fall over. The tumor had been brought on by complications from a demolitions incident in Vietnam. And with that operation, I found out that the Navy didn't want me either.

The doctor who did the operation told me, "Keith, we're going to retire you." I said, "I don't want that." He said, "I'm sorry, you don't have a choice. You can't go back to duty." I wrote my congressman, I wrote the big cahuna of the SEAL teams, the whole nine yards. I begged them to let me stay. It was all I knew.

Their answer was "You're unfit for active duty." They were taking all the steps they could to get rid of the vets in the SEAL teams. Because we were a wild bunch. I know, personally, when I got back I slept with a pistol under my pillow for six months.

I was twenty-eight years old and I thought, "This is wrong. You took us so young and taught us so much and exposed us to so much, and now you want to get rid of the riff-raff." I had to take the retirement. It was like taking nine-and-a-half years out of my life and just saying it never existed.

Then I found out that employers didn't want to have a lot to do with you if you had been medically discharged or medically retired. I could understand their viewpoint, but I could not sit home. I didn't care what it took. I could not stand doing nothing.

I'd learned a lot from my grandfathers while they were alive. One was a finish carpenter and one was a framer. So I could pick up a little work here and there, plus my Navy retirement coming in. I could get by.

My life in the Navy had cost me my first marriage. Unfortunately, there were two children involved. I keep in touch with them. My daughter just turned twenty-three, and my older son will be twenty-one in March. After I divorced, I got caught up in a rebound. I married my youngest son's mother too soon, I know that now. Bobby was born in '81. I've always been close to him, probably because I was there when he was born.

I got divorced a second time in 1986. That one I didn't even know was coming. I guess a lot of it was my fault—the people I run with at work. I mean, we weren't womanizing or anything like that. It was just a typical blue-collar job. You get off work, you go out, you unwind, you have a few beers, you go home.

I don't think I dated for two years after the second divorce. I was working at the post office at the time, and all I did was work and sleep. I didn't know why I worked so much at the time, but I do now—so I didn't have to go home. Then I did start dating again. But I didn't want anything permanent. I didn't want anything obligated. I think I had had enough of obligations in general.

In '89, I developed a friendship with a guy at work who introduced me to Margie, my present wife, at a dance. The more we were around each other, the closer we became. I let the lease go on the house I was renting and moved in with Margie about a year and a half later.

I asked myself, "Do you want to do this? It's an obligation. Are you ready for this?" It took a couple of months to think it out. It seemed like everything was right on the edge, and I was afraid to step over the line. I could go right up to that line, but I couldn't go across it. Fortunately, there was enough feeling there that I ended up going over the line.

I can never express enough gratitude to Margie, because she was there for me when nobody else was. She was willing to take the chance the same as I was. I sat down one night with her early on in our relationship, and I told her everything—the marriages, the problem with drinking, everything.

I told her, "If you say that you don't think you can go through with this relationship, let me know now. I'll understand." She said, "I don't even have to think about it," so that settled that. Yep, she's always been there.

Not even a month after I moved in with Margie, we were unloading catalogs at work and I felt my legs get real tight, like they were drawing up. I thought I had strained a muscle. Next morning, I couldn't get out of bed. Margie had to help me.

I went to see a neurosurgeon. After five months of MRI's, bone scans, and I don't know how many x-rays, they finally found my back was broken. The crack in my spine was so narrow, right where the Navy had taken the tumor out. If I hadn't been in such good physical condition, I would have been paralyzed or dead.

I think the first thing you have to talk about when something like that happens is fear. There's no way to describe the fear of knowing that every day, when you wake up, your legs are getting weaker because you have no feeling in them. I could see the muscles shrinking.

The doctor said I had two choices—an operation or, within six months' time, a wheelchair. There was no choice really, but I'd never faced anything like that in my time in the SEALs. And to face it when I was forty-one, on top of all the other things, was very hard, very degrading. Because I knew what my physical performance levels had been, and when those were taken away from me, it was hard to accept.

The surgery stabilized my back, but it also resulted in my losing seventy-five percent of the feeling in my left leg and sixty percent in my right leg. My legs feel like there's electricity running through them all the time, like I've been sitting on them. Sometimes, if I do too much, I get cramps, and the next morning after the cramps I wake up with bruises.

I can't lie down on the floor anymore, like I used to. I can't wrestle with my son. My workout regimen is practically nil. I can't walk great distances, so hiking is out. I used to love to swim, and I can't do much of that anymore.

At first, it was real hard to put up with emotionally. My natural instinct is, I guess, to push, push, push. I kept pushing myself. Then I got to the point where I could only push so far. You have to learn to accept it, because you can't change it. There are still moments when I want to cut loose and do something, but I know I can't. I have to keep telling myself, "Do you want to suffer for it later? Because you will." So I don't. But the temptation is still there.

The break in my back made it twice that something had happened to me physically that could have either paralyzed me or killed me. But it didn't. And I think that was an indicator to me that I have a purpose in being here. The back problem was telling me I have something to do.

After the surgery, after they had put the pins and the plates in my back, they told me to get on with my life. I was willing to go back to the post office, but the post office wouldn't take me back. This started me thinking. "You're over forty years old. You can't go back to being a common laborer. You physically can't. What do you want to do?" I didn't know.

Then I got into these programs that were supposed to help me. Navy, post office, V.A. programs. Bureaucracy. All the doors shutting in my face. I thought, "There's got to be an answer somewhere. What can I do? How can I get information to help me make up my mind?" Finally, I went to the library, looked through the occupational handbook.

I saw this thing, "counselor." At the bottom of the page it said, "See also *social work*." So I turned to that. I started reading, and the description...It was right there in front of me. I told myself, "This is the answer. This is what you need to do."

In '92, I started going to school through the V.A. Like I said before, I hated high school so bad all I wanted was out. Who would have thought that, twenty-some years later, I'd be dying to get back in? It's amazing. I've learned so much in school already, and I still have another year to go. Then I need to get a master's degree in social work. I'm looking forward to it because I know the end result will be worth the wait.

Two years after I started back to school, Margie and I got married. We were in Las Vegas where they have all these wedding chapels. I had been after her for over a year to marry me. She kept saying, "We'll see, we'll see."

Half jokingly, I said to her, "This is your last chance, kid. I'm going to ask you one more time, and I'm not going to ask you anymore. Do you want to get married?" And she said, "Yes." This marriage has probably been so good for me because I knew her for such a long time. I didn't jump into it headlong like before.

To me, what I'm experiencing now in marriage is what a marriage should be. I have things I like to do. She has things she likes to do. I like rock music, she likes classical—that's okay. We don't try to push each other into things we don't want to do. There's a lot of communication. We listen to each other. She's very supportive of my going to school. I try to be supportive of her in her job.

I think we make a pretty good team. My children, they all think the world of her, and that's important to me. I think they're pretty happy seeing Dad settle down. He's not the wild, crazy guy they remember. It probably has something to do with age. What's that expression? "Mellow with age." It kind of fits.

Now that I'm in my forties, I really think I'm a better person than I was at twenty, maybe because of the things I've experienced. I look at life differently. I know it's more important to me to be able to communicate with my kids than just to say, "This is what I want done." I think the old days of ruling with an iron fist are gone. Communication is probably the key to being a good father nowadays—communication both ways, not just going out, but coming in. After going to school and interacting with the kids at school, I have a better interaction with my own kids.

I think I've also talked more openly with my dad over the last five years than I have in my whole life. We've both kind of changed now. For the better. There's a lot more warmth, and we have things to talk about—fishing, vacationing, other simple things.

Over the last few years, I've made several trips to Arizona. First, I went out there because the weather feels good with my back, but the trips have also made me focus on the work I want to do after I get my degree. I want to work with Native American veterans. On one of my trips, I became aware of some problems the Havasu tribe at Fort McDowell Reservation was having with the government about their right to have gambling on their land, so they can raise money for things like a new community center.

That incident piqued my interest enough that I started going around the reservations and talking to various people. I got kind of a feel for the culture. For example, I found out that Ira Hayes is buried on the Fort McDowell reservation. I had heard of the gentleman, a hero from World War II, who helped raise the flag at Iwo Jima. Well, he's buried behind the tribal council headquarters on the Havasu tribe reservation. And you go back there, and you'd never know it. I mean, it's just a mound of dirt, not a marker, nothing, and the guy was a war hero. And I thought, "Where's the V.A. now? Where's the government now?"

Seeing his grave rang some bells for me. There are numerous veterans on the reservations who have never used their benefits, because they didn't know they had them or because they didn't want to put up with the bureaucratic red tape. I've talked to several people out there, and to my own V.A. representative here, and they've all said there's a need for a coordinator between the Indian veterans and the V.A. That's the position I hope to create. That's my goal.

In the meantime, I've been involved in some volunteer work with the local Native American center. I started out talking with the director of the center. We came around to the subject of alcoholism and Indians. We set up a Tuesday night AA meeting at the center called "Join the Tribe." We read from *The Big Book*, then discuss it.

This work with the Indians is important to me because it puts me in their mindset, gives me their view of things. It's a good background for what I want to do in Arizona. I'm learning some of their customs, their ways of thinking about things, their language.

Doing this work has also taught me a lot about myself. I've learned patience, not to be so quick to anger over the shortcomings of people. I used to be aggressive, defensive. What was emphasized when I was growing up, and in the Navy especially, was "Stand your ground."

When I was younger, I wasn't afraid to speak what was on my mind in any circumstance, to tell somebody off just for the sake of telling somebody off. The anger was also probably a defense mechanism, you know, a way to protect myself so people couldn't get close to me. I always had to have the right answer any time anybody asked me a question.

Native Americans have a tradition of patience. They are aware of the things that are done against them, they protest them, but they know they can't do a lot without patience. What better lesson to be learned from a group of people who live it all the time? I've also learned to be more open, more gentle with people. I've found a gentleness that I never knew I had. I never even considered myself in this way. I know I've come a complete circle from what I was trained as in the Navy. You could say I've gone from warrior to peace-giver.

I always wanted to treat people the way *I* wanted to be treated. I wanted to be accepted, but I never knew how to treat other people gently until I started working around the center. These people accept me for who I am. They don't expect me to be a big hero or have all the answers.

Indians don't ask for much. They just ask for the willingness to give a little. It dawned on me that if you give just a little, you get so much back. So I've learned to give a little, and somebody else gives a little, and it all works out.

Living with Passion

Antonio Pazos

I'm forty-two, and I'm starting to live my life. Before forty, it was a learning process. I did hurt, and I did experience exciting things, but it was just learning. Now that I'm in my forties, things are really happening for me in my career. I feel like now I'm ready—physically, sexually, artistically, intellectually. My life has started to bloom.

Antonio Pazos (his real name), a forty-two-year-old muralist from Tucson, Arizona, views his midlife as the fulfillment of his boyhood dreams. As one of twelve children in a poor Mexican family, becoming an artist was an aspiration he could just barely imagine. Not only did the idea of education seem beyond reach because of the cost, the culture did not encourage his intellectual and artistic direction. When the opportunity to study art presented itself in his late teens, Antonio suffered ridicule from those in his family and community. As a result, he spent much of his young manhood struggling with and breaking through cultural barriers in order to fulfill his dream.

Because his education and career were so hard won, Antonio does not take them for granted. And, just as he did when he was a boy, he protects his commitment to learning and art.

At forty-two, Antonio once again finds himself resisting cultural and parental expectations about being married and having a family. Divorced when he was thirty, he spent the next decade establishing his career.

A series of relationships with women in his thirties, one of whom he came close to marrying, forced him to question his behavior and reevaluate where his real commitment lies. Following his passion has involved making painful choices and redefining the meaning of family in his own way.

Antonio's early midlife has been marked by expanded learning and personal growth. He has been able to draw on the strength of self-determination he developed as a boy and follow his own direction. And his exuberance for life colors his positive outlook on aging.

Antonio greets us at his busy office at the El Rio Community Center in Tucson, Arizona, where he is assistant director, a job that allows him to exercise another value he learned as a boy—helping others. He is a tall, brown-skinned man with very black hair that is just beginning to grey. He is casually dressed in jeans and a red- and blue-checked shirt. His manner is open and unself-conscious, and he is as respectful to the children who wander into his office as he is to the adults.

Antonio's modest office is cluttered with art works and posters of upcoming events at the community center. A map of Mexico hangs on the wall, and a photograph of his parents is prominent on the bulletin board next to his desk.

I was born and raised in Mexico, in Hermosillo, the capital of the state of Sonora, the northernmost state. I remember my mother being pregnant always. There are twelve children. I am the fourth to the oldest. I came to this country when I was twenty-three.

My father will be seventy-one soon. You know, you always want to be like your dad. Especially if your dad happens to be a good example and a good person, which my dad is. Always been a really honest, hard-working man.

My dad has had white hair since he was about forty-five or fifty. He looks very handsome, and I always thought that it was very dignified of him, the way he wore his white hair and the way he wore his wrinkles and everything. He looked like such a strong man, such a beautiful man.

I always said, "When I grow to be my dad's age, I will never dye my hair. I will never try to look like a teenager." At least in our culture, as people are getting older—especially around their forties—they have a tendency to dress younger. I remember some of my uncles doing that, dressing up in brighter colors, really funky, green pants with yellow shirts and so forth. And my dad didn't. My dad was always himself. Even though he was a humble man, humble in financial means, he was always very proud.

Mexican fathers have a tendency to raise macho kids. From the start, our dad taught us how to fight. He would spar with us. I do that with the kids here at the center now. It's something that I learned from my father.

Ever since I was a little kid, my dad would always tease me and hit me in the head, and I'd turn around and try to punch him, and he would block it and hit me. It's funny—you don't realize what's happening until you get into a real fight. Because my dad wouldn't sit and say, "Well, listen, I don't want you to be a pussy. You're going to be a *macho*. I don't want anybody to beat you up." He never said that. He just taught us how to defend ourselves in such a subtle way that we didn't even notice it.

My mother was very religious, and both my parents believed in helping people. We were very, very poor. But if we could share, like, half a piece of bread with someone who didn't have any, we did it happily. Beggars would come to the house, and my mother would give them food. Sometimes the neighbors needed money for medicine. And I don't know how my mother did it, because we were very poor, and there were twelve of us. But the example of helping people, I got it from both my parents. All these values, they sort of stay with you, you know?

Recently, my dad told me he was bothered by the fact that he could never give me the money for my education. I said, "You know what, dad? What is important are the values you gave me. You taught me to be a man, to be an honest person, to be a hard-working, industrious person. You gave me the foundation to be the man that I am. You gave me the tools to build my own future. That's what you gave me, and it's better than money by a long shot." He started crying.

So you ask me what my influences are. There are a lot of people I have admired. I've traveled a good part of the world. I've met people who were very brilliant and very good to me, but I have to say that my father...both my parents, you know, but when it comes to the male figure, it's got to be my dad who's been the most important influence in my life.

Ever since I was a kid, I knew I was different than my brothers and sisters. We had a big yard, and I always used to hang around in the farthest corner all by myself, getting a little mud, doing a little sculpture or whatever. My mom thought there was something wrong with me. My brothers were always fighting and being a royal pain in the ass, always mischievous and getting into trouble. And I wasn't. I was very shy, and I was very calm—always in the corner.

For some reason, education was never a priority in my house. I think it was probably because we were very poor, very humble. I didn't start wearing shoes until I was in third grade. I didn't think there was anything wrong with that. All my friends, we were all poor the same. I never saw any other way of life, so it was all real normal to me, and it was no big deal. But I think that's why education was never really pushed, like the way I push my own daughter. I never heard from my dad, "You're going to go to college." It was "As soon as you can, you got to start looking for a job."

After I graduated from high school, my dad found me a job, and I was fairly happy with it at first. But then it came to a point where I said to myself, "I'm really not very happy."

I was working as a surveyor's helper measuring the coastline of Mexico. I spent over a year living at the seashore, camping out. I liked that because I love the ocean. But come on! You know? What about culture? What about music? What about people? I was there pretty much by myself.

That was a turning point in my life because the year-and-a-half I spent camping by the ocean I had a lot of time on my hands, a lot of time to think and make a decision. As young as I was, I had always known that I wanted to be an artist. But I didn't know how to do it. When that job at the ocean was finished, I said, "I don't want to do this anymore. I want to go back to school."

For me, it was difficult to get into being an artist, even going to the university. We all have dreams when we're growing up, especially in our teenage years. My greatest dream was to go to art school and learn how to draw. And that's it. I didn't think about graduating. Didn't think about scholarship. None of that stuff. I could never, ever imagine seeing myself in Paris lecturing at the Sorbonne, or teaching in the States, or exhibiting in Zurich and Morocco. Never. Because my dreams were so limited. All I ever wanted to do was be in a place where I could learn how to draw. That's it.

One day, after I had decided I wanted to go back to school, I was passing by the academy of fine arts in my home town. To me, it was such a big thing to imagine being there. I used to look up at the building with awe. So I was just looking inside the place, and a priest who worked there said, "What are you looking at?" I said, "Oh, I'm sorry. I'm just looking." He said, "No, that's all right, come in."

He walked me into the art class and introduced me to the art teacher. We talked for a little bit, and the teacher kept drawing words out of my mouth because I wouldn't say anything. "Do you like art?" "Uh, yes." "Can you draw?" "A little." I guess the teacher noticed that I was very nervous. But I was nervous because I liked it so much.

For four months after that, I thought about going to the academy. I had to work up the nerve to go back. I wondered, "How am I going to do it? What am I going to say?" Every day when I would wake up, I would think about the day I was going to go see this teacher.

So one day I did it. I told the teacher, "I don't have any money." He said, "No problem." He gave me a piece of paper, some sort of scholarship or fee waiver. So I signed up for two classes at the academy. I couldn't believe it.

I was really crazy about it, but my family wasn't. My family and friends were, like, "What are you, stupid or something?" They said, "Fine arts are for weird people." I thought, "I'm not weird." But they had all these macho things, and they thought it was funny that I would sit down and make little drawings of things.

I remember a lot of pressure from my neighbors, my friends, my family. I can still feel it, even now. It was a very hard time. It made me very angry that the traditions of society were so much against me. But I got over it, little by little.

Then, out of the blue, this couple who had plenty of money asked me to teach them how to draw and play the guitar. That was my first job, really. He owned a store, and he would pay me with eggs and cheese and chickens and beans. Every day they would give me something to take home. I would take it to my house, and my mom would be very happy.

And then my drawings started getting better, and they started selling. I think the first drawing I sold brought in about $90 back then. So my parents, little by little, started to see that I was on the right track, that I was different in what I wanted to do, but that it was paying off.

After that, I got a scholarship to come study in the States. My parents were very, very worried about me because they knew I was a fairly shy kid. They wondered, "What is this kid going to do in this strange country? He doesn't even speak English." The people at the university who were going to give me the scholarship asked me if I spoke English. I said, "Sure I do." I didn't really. I just wanted the scholarship. I didn't know how I was going to do it. I just wanted to come to school.

I wanted to learn so much. I never thought in terms of achieving, or making money, or being famous—I just wanted to learn, to see how it's done. I had a great deal of curiosity. The university was very good to me, and my grades, of course, were excellent.

On my way back to Mexico after I graduated, I stopped by this very community center to visit some friends who were working here. They told me the center needed a muralist, and since I didn't have a reason to go back to Hermosillo, I figured I'd stay here for the summer and do the mural. While I was working on the mural project, the people from Pima College asked me if I would stay and teach art classes. Then they offered me a job here at El Rio Community Center.

Once I had established myself in Tucson, I got married and had a child with her, a little girl. She's thirteen now. A very talented little girl, very pretty and very good-hearted.

The marriage didn't last. The marriage was an unfortunate thing, I think, for both of us. We were both inexperienced, and rather young. My little girl was almost three when I left. I was thirty when we divorced.

After that, of course, it was really rough times. I had left cars, furniture, house, money, all that stuff behind me. And I had to support my little girl and the house even though I didn't live there.

I had a really hard time personally, too, because I thought I had done everything by the book—the way I had been taught to do it. Be patient, be cool, don't get angry, don't argue in front of the kids—just like my parents. I felt really bad because I had always wanted to be like my dad, you know? But I couldn't, because I didn't have the marriage that he had. I felt that I had let my dad down.

One of the things I was never able to understand or live with was the fact that my little girl was being kept away from me. I didn't see her for eight months. Me and my little girl are really tight. There's a very strong bond between us. So when they kept my little girl away from me during the divorce proceedings and afterwards, it was really tough. I was so miserable. That was probably the worst experience I've ever had. And I know that she hurt as much as I did, if not more.

So that's the only thing I regret about the divorce. Otherwise, I feel it's the best thing I've ever done. Because my career took off after that, and today I am very happy.

I was extremely curious about who I was after I had gone through all the hurting and the different changes. Before I got married, I had known who I was and what I wanted to do, but for some reason I thought marriage and having kids was more important than my career. After the divorce, I was ready to take more chances, to be more daring.

My first trip to Europe, when I was thirty-eight, was very important to me because I found out that I could travel and make friends and connections. I found that people were ready to help me and take on commitments alongside me—exhibitions, lectures at the University of Paris, conferences, that sort of thing.

My self-esteem really improved a great deal. I was published in French by University Books, and that made me feel pretty good. Then my artwork started to improve as well, and things just really started to fall into place. So I feel energized. I feel very good about my hunches and what I can do. Now that I'm in my forties, I think I can take on better and bigger things. I feel comfortable with my growth, and about what I've learned from what I've gone through.

I was invited to exhibit in Europe. Eventually, I was invited to go there and lecture in Paris. Then, from there, came other lectures, other universities, other exhibitions. And every time I came back to Tucson from a European trip, there was more work. People were more interested in what I had done and what I had learned.

When I was still living in Mexico in my twenties, I did abstract painting and sculpture because I thought it was the thing to do. But after I came to the States, I started to see things from a different point of view. I started looking into myself, into my culture, my own blood, my own race, into who I really was. I took off my mask. I said, "There it is. You're brown. This is who you are. That's it."

I started to see that my abstract aspirations were so incredibly shallow. And then I looked inside myself, and I saw a lot of strength—the strength of my culture. And I thought, "I can actually go back into my own past at least 2,000 years." You know? Trace back the history of Mexico, and the civilizations of the Aztecs and the Mayans.

I started digging deeper into that and devouring books about my culture, and getting those dates and styles of terra cotta or painting or murals into my head. I was a pretty happy person as I discovered myself and my culture.

This strong cultural identity and knowledge is what most people like to see in my work and hear about in my lectures. Five years ago, I painted a 25-by-60-foot-long mural about the history of Mexico that hangs now in the Tucson Museum of Art. I like to portray the people of the past, the people of the present—but as they are, not from a romantic, paternalistic view of the Mexican Indian, not Mexican-souvenir type work. The reality of their lives, the suffering, the struggle—all these experiences portrayed in portraits and settings of people doing ordinary things. I paint the people with dignity, dignity that they themselves don't even know they have, pride that they don't even know they have. So when an Indian looks at my picture, he'll say, "That's who I am."

I paint what I live and what I see around me. I work in this neighborhood center, and I see poverty, I see injustice, I see racism, I see people who are really hungry. I see a lot of need around here. Drug abuse. It hurts deeply. Little kids going to waste. Whole families going down. I mean, these kids have two or three brothers in jail. It's really hard. When I live in an atmosphere like this, I can't turn my back and say I want to draw little pictures of flowers.

As assistant director of the center, I'm in charge of cultural affairs and recreational programs. I want to motivate the kids to have a better life, to have an education, to stay away from drugs. The things that worry me are part of who I am.

Something that bothers me at this point in my life is that I've had a lot of relationships since the divorce. A lot of them—too many, I think. And that started to bother me as well, that I had too many female friends. Somehow it seemed to me that every relationship became serious, that the women expected marriage from me because I had been divorced for so long. Or maybe I misled them. I'm not really sure.

It upset me a great deal that I couldn't settle down, that I couldn't have one woman who would be my girlfriend, that I couldn't make a commitment. I could never really be stable in that manner. I kept going from one relationship to another.

I kept hurting women, and therefore I suffered a great deal, too. You have no idea how much I've cried over these things. Because I'm supposed to be the kind of person who helps people, always doing whatever is needed for people, and then I'm hurting someone like this. I don't know, maybe something is wrong with me. I still haven't figured it out.

Not long ago I was going to marry someone I thought was perfect for me. She was an exceptional woman. She was from my hometown, the woman that my mother had always told me to marry, you know what I mean? My parents raised me to look for a woman like this. And then she comes along, and she is beautiful, very honest, very religious, very intelligent. She had everything. I was pretty happy with her. She treated me extremely well, just like my mom treats my dad.

But then I came to the realization that I didn't want her to treat me like my mom treats my dad. It bothered me that she didn't have her own life and career, that she was not her own individual, that I was everything for her. She used to tell me that. You know, Mexican women can be very romantic and extremely passionate—to a fault.

So when it was time to get married, just weeks away from it, I changed my mind. And of course, she was deeply hurt and so were her parents and my parents. And I said to myself, "What the hell's the matter with me? Why can't I just do it and live with it? That's a pretty important aspect of my life." That really worries me at this point.

Culturally, there are certain values that make you a "real man," a "man of worth." One of them—among others, like honesty and dignity and respect—is family. All of my other brothers and sisters have done like my parents. They're married. They have children. So even though I'm very comfortable most of the time with being single, this is always going to be in the back of my mind as something that I have not accomplished.

What I have come to terms with is that I'm not going to marry any woman because I *should.* Or because I'm forty-two and I think I should find somebody. Without a doubt, my career is a priority. But if a midlife crisis is coming, it will have nothing to do with my career. It will be about my relationships.

A friend told me that I don't need a family in the normal sense because I have my art. Every piece of art, every mural has a child in it and is going to be there forever. And at the community center, I have all these kids around me who respect my opinion. That explanation felt right to me.

Like when I was in Paris for the summer, I came back and the kids were very happy to see me, but then they started crying. I said, "Why are you crying?" They told me that Joseph, one of the kids that hung out at the center, had been killed. His brother was playing with a .38 gun and shot him in the head. I cried for days. It still bothers me that I wasn't here. That's when I started to feel that this really is my family, because I worry about them on a day-to-day basis. I'm aware of what they're going through.

In my thirties, I did a great deal of reflection and looking inside myself, trying to be honest about who I really am. The marriage thing didn't work for me, and I've learned to live with that. I've learned to feel comfortable with that because what I do in my career is enough.

I'm forty-two, and I'm starting to live my life. Before forty, it was a learning process. I did hurt, and I did experience exciting things, but it was just learning. Now that I'm in my forties, things are really happening for me in my career. I feel like now I'm ready—physically, sexually, artistically, intellectually. My life has really started to bloom.

I'm still very, very curious. I take classes in Paris when I go there to lecture. I go and visit people, and I learn from them. This learning thing is a big thing with me. My apartment is full of books. I cannot waste one hour of my life without learning something new. I have a great desire to learn and to live as much as possible with great passion.

I believe that the more you live, the better artist you'll be. That's imbedded in my head and my heart. I'm a great admirer of Matisse and Picasso and other people who lived so long and were so creative. So, believe it or not, I'm actually looking forward to when I'm sixty or seventy or eighty.

My family thinks I'm crazy when I tell them this. But I have no doubt in my mind about it—in the same way I knew I was going to be an artist when I was a kid. It was just *in* me, that no matter what happens, no matter what the family, what society or the whole world says, I'm going to be what I am.

I know when I'm older I'm going to be somewhere creating artwork, making murals, sculpture, or whatever. All that I'm learning and doing and seeing, it's for those days. From this point on it's up, not down. I feel very young still because I'm learning so much, and that's an attitude I want to keep.

I think that's why I feel this desire to live and do things and go different places. I want to experience life. I think that's why I feel so good about being forty-two. If this is midlife, midlife is wonderful. Give me more!

Bibliography

Betcher, William, and Pollack, William. *In a Time of Fallen Heroes: The Re-Creation of Masculinity.* New York: Macmillan Publishing Company, 1993.

Bly, Robert. *Iron John: A Book About Men.* Reading, MA: Addison-Wesley Publishing Company, 1990.

Fanning, Patrick, and McKay, Matthew. *Being a Man: A Guide to the New Masculinity.* Oakland, CA: New Harbinger Publications, 1993.

Farrel, Michael P., and Rosenberg, Stanley D. *Men at Midlife.* Boston: Suburn House Publishing Company, 1981.

Gerzon, Mark. *Coming Into Our Own: Understanding the Adult Metamorphosis.* New York: Delacorte Press, 1992.

Gilmore, David D. *Manhood in the Making: Cultural Concepts of Masculinity.* New Haven: Yale University Press, 1990.

Harding, Christopher. *Wingspan: Inside the Men's Movement.* New York: St. Martin's Press, 1992.

Lenfest, David. *Men Speak Out: In the Heart of Men's Recovery.* Deerfield Beach, FL: Health Communications, 1991.

Levinson, Daniel J. *The Seasons of a Man's Life.* New York: Ballantine Books, 1978.

Moore, Thomas. *Care of the Soul.* New York: HarperCollins, 1992.

Pasick, Robert. *Awakening from the Deep Sleep: A Powerful Guide for Courageous Men.* San Francisco: HarperCollins, 1992.

Pittman, Frank. *Man Enough: Fathers, Sons, and the Search for Masculinity.* New York: G.P. Putnam's Sons, 1993.

Sanford, John A., and Lough, George. *What Men Are Like.* New York: Paulist Press, 1988.

Male Survivors: *A 12-Step Recovery Program for Survivors of Childhood Sexual Abuse*
"Male Survivors is more than a workbook; it is a courageous personal statement by a deeply religious man. Timothy Sanders provides clear and compassionate guidance to male survivors who wish to choose a spiritual 12-Step program as a frame-work for their recovery."—Mike Lew
By Tim Sanders, M.S.
$12.95 · Paper · 0-89594-485-5

Mavericks of the Mind: *Conversations for the New Millennium*
Interviews by David Jay Brown and Rebecca McClen Novick
Seventeen exceptional men and women reveal decidedly original thoughts about subjects as divers as chaos theory, sexuality, and extraterrestrials.
$12.95 · Paper · 0-89594-601-7

Voices from the Edge: *Conversations with Jerry Garcia, Ram Dass, Annie Sprinkle, Matthew Fox, Jaron Lanier, and Others*
Co-authored by David Jay Brown and Rebecca McClen Novick
Some of the most challenging innovators of our day speak with clarity, insight, and wit on topics such as technology, virtual reality, sexuality, music, space exploration, psychedelics, body piercing, factory farming, spirituality, and death.
$14.95 · Paper · 0-89594-732-3

Men Are from Detroit, Women Are from Paris: *Cartoons by Women*
Edited by Roz Warren
What do women really think about men? More than twenty women cartoonists share their hilarious observations in Roz Warren's latest collection.
$8.95 · Paper · 0-89594-748-X

Sports Injuries: *A Self-Help Guide*
By Vivian Grisogono
An accessible, fully illustrated, easy-to-read manual. Indispensable not only to men and women of all ages, but also to coaches, P.E. teachers, and medical and paramedical practitioners.
$16.95 · Paper · 0-89594-716-1

Growing Old Disgracefully: *New Ideas for Getting the Most Out of Life*
By The Hen Co-op
You are never too old to live life with self-esteem and playfulness. Written by six women between the ages of sixty-four and seventy-seven, this book challenges stereotypes and suggests ways to make life at any age more joyous and creative.
$12.95 · Paper · 0-89594-672-6

Disgracefully Yours: *More New Ideas for Getting the Most Out of Life*
By The Hen Co-op
Members of The Hen Co-op respond to letters form readers of their first book, *Growing Old Disgracefully*. These six vibrant women inspire other women to transform their attitudes toward aging and take the path toward expansion, playfulness, and creativity.
$14.95 · Paper · 0-89594-804-4

To order, please see your local bookstore

To receive a current catalog from
The Crossing Press
please call toll-free,
800-777-1048.